Literature Links
Activities for Gifted Readers

Teresa Smith Masiello

Great Potential Press, Inc.
Scottsdale, Arizona
www.giftedbooks.com

Copy Editor: Jen Ault Rosso
Cover Design/Layout: M W Velgos Design
Cover Photo: Anne Morales
Interior Design/Layout: The Printed Page

Published by
Great Potential Press, Inc.
P.O. Box 5057
Scottsdale, AZ 85261

Printed and bound in the United States of America

Library of Congress Cataloging-in-Publication Data

Masiello, Teresa Smith, 1962-
Literature links: activities for gifted readers / Teresa Smith Masiello.
p. cm.
Includes bibliographical references.
ISBN 0-910707-72-3 (pbk.)
1. Reading (Elementary)—Activity programs. 2. Literature—Study and teaching (Elementary) 3. Gifted children—Books and reading. I. Title.
LB1573.M3757 2005
371.95'34—dc22
2005014878

ISBN 0-910707-72-3

Dedication

This book is dedicated to my mom and dad.
Their strength is like the mighty oak tree.

Acknowledgments

The creation of *Literature Links* would not be possible if not for the efforts, inspirations, and guidance of many individuals. My parents, Marshall and Cecilia Smith, taught me long ago to follow my dreams, to be persistent, and to always trust in my abilities. Their commitment to education allowed me to reach my goal of becoming a teacher. Over the years, I watched my parents battle major illnesses with great dignity. Observing them overcome such challenges inspired me to approach problems with faith and confidence. I am grateful to my parents for believing in me and for being my friends.

Acknowledging my husband, Paul, seems impossible to do in only a couple of sentences. His love and support allowed me to take chances and to further my education. He is patient, kind, and dedicated to his family. His love and guidance always brightens my cloudy days.

My children, Anthony, Jacob, and Nicole are my treasures. My time with them is precious. It is their trust in me that completes my life. My children continue to teach me things that I never learned in the classroom. Our family bond enables each of us to be strong, faithful, and content.

Many thanks must be given to Jim Webb, Janet Gore, and the staff at Great Potential Press. Their belief in me and my ideas is greatly appreciated. The experience of working with such talented publishers, editors, and educators will never be forgotten. This journey has just begun, and I owe everyone who touched this book in so many different ways. Thanks to all who have helped me grow professionally as well as spiritually.

Contents

Preface

Nineteen years ago, I walked into a brand new, freshly painted, kindergarten classroom bedecked (festooned, resplendent, carefully arranged) with letters of the alphabet above the chalkboard; bulletin boards showing off shapes, colors, and numbers; tiny little desks with little chairs neatly tucked under in perfect rows. In one corner, a play kitchen with a stove and refrigerator made little children's eyes beam with excitement. A water table nearby invited 24 eager, curious kindergarteners to investigate. Surely, this room was a perfect setting for learning and fun.

For a while, learning in the bright new room *was* fun—even when I found myself focusing on "following directions," "washing hands," and "walking in line." But by the time fall turned to winter, the smiling bright-eyed little sponges began showing signs of restlessness. The basal readers I depended upon for reading instruction, while providing adequate support for alphabet recognition and basic sight words, were simply not enough for my more advanced readers.

One day, a little girl, not much taller than my waist, asked, "Ms. Smith, when are we going to read real stories, like the ones on the shelves?" My education classes had not prepared me for students who needed more than grade-level instruction—children who were precocious readers.

At that moment, my philosophy and beliefs about teaching changed. I decided to begin anew—with books on the shelves—with real LITERATURE.

This book will tell you how I did it.

Introduction

These are exciting times in which to be educators. Teachers are being asked to depart from textbook teaching and take back control of the curriculum....

—Carol Hurst

Do you have students in your classrooms reading above grade level? Do you ever hear the word "bored" in parent/teacher conferences? Are you searching for innovative reading strategies? Would you like to enhance your reading program? This book will provide ideas and solutions for all the above.

Diversity Dictates Differentiation

Today's classrooms contain students with diverse reading abilities. Students who read below grade level receive support services to improve their skills. Children who read above grade level usually do not receive extra support services because they are able to easily keep up with assignments. A lack of teacher attention and work with adequate challenge, however, can cause bright and gifted students to become frustrated and sometimes bored. They may act out their impatience in class, display anger when assignments appear too easy, and show decreased enthusiasm for reading. The good news is that problem behaviors like these can be avoided if teachers take steps to ensure that the needs of their advanced or gifted readers are met.

Taking Back Control of the Curriculum

Today's teachers feel out of control. They find themselves frustrated by the current emphasis on the federal *No Child Left Behind Act*, in addition to state and local requirements to meet mandated standards. They say:

"We can't extend the curriculum. There's no time."

"I feel I don't have much control over my curriculum. It is totally driven by state standards."

> *"Differentiation is a wonderful concept, but I can't accomplish all of the state requirements and differentiate instruction, too."*

This feeling of being out of control is unfortunate. Most schools have creative, energetic teachers who want to provide an education for all students by designing a curriculum that can be individualized. Is it possible for teachers to take back control of their curriculum and still meet the mandated requirements? The answer is YES.

Most classrooms are equipped with state- or school district-adopted reading textbooks—often called basal readers—that provide a scope and sequence of skills for all students to accomplish. When teachers get "locked in" to using pre-selected titles and activities generated by these textbooks, they begin to lose control of the curriculum. Conversely, when they depart from "total textbook teaching," they can begin, even enthusiastically, to regain some control over the instruction in their classrooms.

It *is* possible to have this kind of flexibility while still meeting the requirements established by state and local school districts. The chapters that follow offer some practical ways to use basal texts as well as trade books in reading programs.

Trade Books in the Classroom

The use of trade books in the classroom can enhance students' learning by adding depth to the curriculum and by providing pathways for students to increase their knowledge and skills (Reis, Gubbins, & Richards, 2002). High-quality trade books are more likely than basal texts to broaden students' knowledge and to provide the challenge and complexity that gifted children need. Gunning (1992) supports the use of trade books with gifted readers by stressing the importance of providing gifted readers with challenging books that promote intellectual growth. He recommends choosing fiction books that contain interesting characters involved in intriguing plots.

Before choosing specific books, teachers need to understand that gifted readers often possess unique characteristics and needs. For example, gifted students tend to read earlier than average-ability children. Some of them read independently at the age of four or five; some read as early as two and three. Rather than being "taught," many of these gifted readers seem to pick up their skills simply by asking their parents and caregivers questions about words and letters or by watching children's television shows like *Sesame Street*.

Once they are able to read independently, Judith Halsted (2002) notes that young gifted readers read a wide variety of books and for longer periods of time. Barbara Clark (2002) notes that because gifted readers have abundant curiosity and interests in many areas, they need exposure to a variety of subjects and issues. With their advanced verbal skills, they should be given opportunities to use increasingly difficult vocabulary and concepts, as well as chances to discuss ideas and viewpoints with others. When teachers understand gifted children's advanced learning characteristics and needs, they will be able to incorporate reading strategies more effectively into their curriculum.

This book will help teachers understand gifted readers better. It encourages teachers to pre-test advanced students in order to skip work already mastered, and it shows them how to move gifted readers through an accelerated reading program while at the same time providing opportunities for students to think critically and creatively. The strategies in this book will please parents, teachers, and students.

What Parents Want from a Reading Program

Parents, teachers, and students all have certain expectations from a reading program. Parents of gifted children voice these concerns:

"My child says she is bored during reading time in school."

"My son wants to read books from the library that are more challenging than the books in the classroom."

"My daughter really wants to discuss stories. She wants to ask questions and talk about the characters."

Parents want their bright children to:

➤ be challenged.
➤ maintain a love of learning through reading.
➤ learn life-long reading skills.
➤ meet characters in books who struggle with the same issues as the gifted child.

What Teachers Want from a Reading Program

Teachers have these concerns:

"My gifted readers seem unhappy and bored during reading time."

"My advanced readers have shut down and will not read from their reading books."

"When I give my gifted readers different novels to read, they still don't seem happy."

"Some of my better readers don't want to do 'other' activities because they don't want their friends to know they are 'different.'"

Teachers want:

➤ activities that can be implemented easily and within time restraints.
➤ material to fit the needs of advanced readers without making other students feel inferior.
➤ a reading program that incorporates a variety of literature to satisfy the different interests of students in their classrooms.
➤ reading programs and activities that contain assessment tools to help evaluate the progress of gifted readers.

What Gifted Readers Want from a Reading Program

Gifted readers themselves have thoughts and opinions about reading:

> *"I wish I had more time to read books in school. I usually read more at home."*

> *"I like to read stories that teach me about real things and real people."*

> *"I sit and read from my library book during reading. I wish we could read library books and then talk about those stories. That would be so cool."*

Student responses tell us that gifted readers want more "meat" and more "meaning" in their reading program. It is time to start listening. When we integrate quality literature and appropriate trade books into reading instruction, we are addressing both academic and social/emotional needs of gifted readers.

How *Literature Links* Will Help

> *Teachers require support and strategies to challenge advanced readers at their highest readiness level.*
> —Bertie Kingore

Meeting the needs of administrators, parents, and students is a challenge for the teacher. This book provides a sequential approach to guiding accelerated readers in the classroom. It contains practical lesson plans and activities that use trade books. Lessons are designed so that *all* students receive differentiated instruction and *no* students will feel different from their friends. *Literature Links* is designed to meet the needs of parents, teachers, and most importantly, gifted students.

Student Objectives

When high-ability learners read the trade books recommended in this book and complete the corresponding activities, they will accomplish several objectives. These students will:

- ➤ gain a better understanding of differences in people and cultures.
- ➤ relate to gifted characters and the issues and conflicts found in the books.
- ➤ increase self-acceptance and self-knowledge.
- ➤ increase reading comprehension skills, such as making inferences, interpreting text, making predictions, and noticing the author's style and use of language.
- ➤ identify and analyze problems that they encounter in stories.
- ➤ evaluate solutions chosen by characters in the stories.
- ➤ read and comprehend material appropriate to individual ability levels.

Teacher Objectives

When teachers use the suggested activities from this book in their classrooms, they will gain valuable skills and insight. Teachers will:

➤ recognize that gifted readers are able to read and learn material at a faster pace.
➤ recognize the need for trade books in reading programs
➤ learn how to adjust material for readers who learn differently.
➤ implement reading strategies that will ensure that gifted readers reach their full potential.
➤ utilize a variety of assessment tools to monitor student progress.
➤ provide an effective communication system between parents, students, and educators.

Parent Objectives

When teachers use the ideas in this book for planning and implementing literature in their classroom, they will satisfy parent wishes for their children. Parents will:

➤ notice increased enthusiasm from their children toward reading.
➤ see differentiated reading strategies.
➤ note progress made by their children in reading.
➤ receive information about the reading program through several communication tools.
➤ have input into their child's education.

Suggestions for Using this Book

The following suggestions will help you integrate strategies from this book into your reading program. Teachers may choose to use the activities for an entire week or for just a few hours. The components of each chapter may be used flexibly.

To integrate literature into thematic instruction. Scan the contents of this book, make a brief list of titles that relate to specific themes, and then match those themes with topics in your basal text. If your basal text has a story that relates to Hispanic culture but is too easy for your advanced readers, allow gifted readers to work with *Abuela,* by Arthur Dorros, while the rest of the class works in the basal text.

To encourage interest-based learning. Administer interest inventories to your advanced readers. For example, use *The Gifted Education Planner: Inventories and Data Collection Forms* (Rogers, 2002b). Locate stories from this book or your library that fit or enhance interests documented on student surveys. Use activities from this book to supplement reading.

To meet students' individual social and emotional needs. Use titles found in this book to help gifted readers who may be struggling with personal social or emotional issues. For example, if you have a student who is struggling with being different from others, you could replace reading instruction from the basal text with the story *Nothing's Fair in Fifth Grade,* by Barthe DeClements. The student could read this story and complete the accompanying activities or have a one-on-one discussion with you about the book.

To find relevant information rapidly. Put tabs on particular pages after you have scanned this book. Your tabs might read "Self-Esteem," "Creative Thinking," or "Small Group Activities."

To have a ready supply of activities for differentiation. Scan Chapters 3 and 4. Highlight strategies you find helpful. Keep a file folder of photocopied activities for use whenever needed.

To avoid teaching students what they already know. Always pre-test prior to starting a new unit. Then use activities from this book to replace unnecessary curriculum for gifted readers.

Occasionally, questions may arise as to why you are using trade books in your classroom. You can answer those questions by saying:

> *"I provide gifted readers with opportunities to show their understanding*
> *of given material and subjects, and then I move them forward using*
> *trade books and activities that meets their individual needs."*

Chapter 1
Understanding the Gifted Reader

Most reading programs, whether traditional or literature based, have failed to meet the learning needs of many different gifted students. Most high ability students have already mastered the vocabulary and skills they will be expected to "learn" this year.

—Susan Winebrenner

Who Are Gifted Readers?

Before teachers can effectively use trade books with gifted learners, they must understand the characteristics and needs of these learners. How would you answer the following questions posed by well-known reading teacher and presenter Bertie Kingore (2002a)? You may wish to write your answers in a notebook or journal and add new ideas or fresh understandings as they come to you.

Questions to Help Teachers Focus on Gifted Readers

➤ What does the term "advanced reader" or "gifted reader" mean to you?
➤ How do you identify "advanced potential in reading"?
➤ What instructional needs are unique to advanced children?
➤ Does your school challenge advanced children academically? If so, how?
➤ What social and emotional issues are critical when challenging advanced readers?
➤ What are some behavioral concerns and implications for gifted students?
➤ What grouping considerations should we address for gifted students?
➤ What resources—human and material—can we draw upon?
➤ What additional resources might we need?
➤ How might we involve parents in a learning partnership?

Definition and Characteristics of Gifted Readers

Children who demonstrate exceptional ability in reading and working with text information are considered gifted readers (Mason & Au, 1990). These children display a host of characteristics. They tend to:

➤ read earlier and more independently than other children their age.
➤ read longer than other students and often read a variety of literature (Halsted, 2002).
➤ learn material faster and are able to deal with complex and abstract issues.
➤ have an intense passion in multiple topics (Winebrenner, 2001).
➤ take responsibility for constructive meaning using prior knowledge.
➤ think strategically, plan and monitor their comprehension, and revise their strategies.
➤ have confidence that they are effective learners.

Susannah Richards (2002) provides additional characteristics of talented readers. She suggests that teachers look for students who understand nuances of language. Look for students who:

➤ use more than one strategy when creating meaning.
➤ read far beyond their chronological age.
➤ enjoy reading various types of material.
➤ look at books to help solve problems.
➤ want to choose their own books to read.
➤ relate literature to their own lives.

Teachers who plan to differentiate reading instruction for gifted readers should begin by noticing and then identifying these students' characteristics and needs. Only after fully understanding *who the gifted readers are* can educators respond effectively to *what these gifted readers need.*

Gifted Readers Speak Out

Reading is fun. I even like it when my teacher reads to our class. We sit on the floor and my teacher reads to us after lunch. We get to talk about the books with our friends.

     —first-grade student

I wish we had more time to read books in school. I usually read more at home.

     —second-grade student

I like to read stories that teach me about real things and real people. I guess I like history books the best.

     —third-grade student

What Do Gifted Readers Need?

Determining and defining the specific needs of the talented reader is crucial to effective teaching. If the learning needs of gifted readers are not met, this population of students can easily lose interest or become frustrated. They may find other (sometimes non-productive) ways to entertain themselves, such as acting out in class, being the class clown, or daydreaming during scheduled reading times.

Barbara Clark (1983) states that gifted readers have the following needs:

➤ to be exposed to new and challenging information about the environment and the culture.

➤ to be exposed to varied subjects and concerns.

➤ to be allowed to pursue ideas as far as their interests take them.

➤ to encounter and use increasingly different vocabulary and concepts.

➤ to be exposed to ideas appropriate to the individual rate of learning.

➤ to pursue inquiries beyond allotted time spans.

Gifted readers need opportunities to reflect on the text being read, and they need to summarize main ideas and themes while evaluating conflicts and solutions presented in literature. In addition, reading instruction for gifted readers needs to link new material to prior knowledge and experiences.

Problems that May Accompany Giftedness

What happens if the needs of gifted readers are not met? Experts such as May Seagoe (1974), Barbara Clark (2002), and James T. Webb (1994) have all developed lists of characteristics of gifted children that help teachers understand their subsequent learning needs. The following chart of characteristics and possible problems, adapted from Webb (1994), helps us understand common traits of gifted students and illustrates how those very traits can sometimes lead to problems in classrooms or in other environments.

Characteristics	Possible Problems
Acquires and retains information easily	May become impatient with others; often dislikes basic routines
Inquisitive; searches for significance	Sometimes asks embarrassing questions
Intrinsic motivation; self-motivated	Strong-willed; resists direction
Enjoys problem solving; able to conceptualize; questions teaching procedures	May resist routine
Seeks cause-and-effect relationships	Dislikes unclear or illogical areas like traditions and feelings
Emphasizes truth, equity, and fair play	Exhibits worries about humanitarian concerns
Tries to organize things and people	Constructs complicated rules; sometimes viewed as being bossy
Large vocabulary	May use words to manipulate
Likes new ways of doing things	May be seen as disruptive

Reviewing these characteristics of gifted children and the potential problems that each can lead to helps us to understand why gifted students need special consideration. For example, when we realize that gifted children are often self-motivated and dislike routine or strong directives, we can understand that they need opportunities to choose some of the things that they might like to do or learn. And when we see that they generally have an advanced vocabulary, we understand why it is important to offer reading material with challenging vocabulary. Knowing that gifted students possess specific needs can also help us understand that problems such as off-task behaviors can arise if the academic, social, and emotional needs of gifted readers are not met.

We have all heard phrases like this one: "He can't be gifted; he never finishes his work." Perhaps we have said it ourselves. But that gifted child may simply not be interested or challenged; the work may be too easy—and therefore boring—for him. Without challenge, gifted children often learn to underachieve. If everything is too easy for them, they may never learn how to study—a skill they will need to have in high school and college.

"She has temper tantrums; she's immature. I don't think she could be gifted." A young child can be frustrated by having to sit and wait through instruction on material and information that she already knows. Or a young gifted child may be impatient—unable to understand why other children don't learn as quickly as she. All of the above are cases in which a teacher may not realize that the problem behavior is due to the child's gifted ability rather than an intent to be disrespectful.

"She seems smart, but her handwriting is totally illegible." Or, "He may be bright, but he sure doesn't get along well with other children." Teachers who understand the characteristics of gifted children will be able to help. Gifted children often show uneven development. Handwriting uses fine motor skills; advanced ability in mathematics uses advanced abstract reasoning. While a child's understanding of mathematics may be quite advanced, his handwriting has not caught up (and may never catch up). A child may not get along with others because she may not have much in common with age peers. If she likes chess but other fourth-grade girls prefer to talk about clothes, then she may appear to not get along with them.

There are many misconceptions about gifted children, and one of these is that they are gifted in everything. Teachers may overlook gifted readers because they do not display gifted characteristics in other subject areas. A third-grade teacher asked me to come and observe a youngster in her classroom. After a few weeks of observation and reviewing records, I discussed the possibility that this student might be gifted or advanced in reading. The teacher said, "She can't be gifted in reading; she has a B in math and science." I explained that students are not typically gifted in all areas, which sometimes causes them to not be labeled as gifted in any area. Regardless of whether a child has the "gifted" label, advanced readers deserve opportunities to be challenged. A student like the one mentioned above should be given the opportunity to "test out" of slow-paced curriculum and move forward at her own pace in reading to ensure that learning is achieved.

Identifying Gifted Readers

It is apparent that finding and identifying gifted readers becomes extremely important in order to properly meet their needs. Take a look at the identification checklists on the following pages.

Checklist for Identifying Strong Readers

Teacher Directions: *Check all statements below that apply. If the student receives 15 or more indicators, supplement and differentiate the student's reading by using trade books.*

Name:_____Date: _____Teacher:_____	

1. Student brings knowledge to a topic. _____

2. Student uses advanced vocabulary. _____

3. Student reads fluently. _____

4. Student comprehends what is read. _____

5. Student responds to a book in many ways. _____

6. Student asks questions when faced with an "unknown." _____

7. Student wants to read during free time. _____

8. Student reflects on a book through verbal communication and writing. _____

9. Student feels good after reading. _____

10. Student understands the purpose of reading. _____

11. Student uses appropriate "self-correcting" strategies as he/she reads. _____

12. Student spends most of his/her time reading at home. _____

13. Student is able to skim and scan. _____

14. Student predicts outcomes. _____

15. Student uses context clues. _____

16. Student often searches for text sense. _____

17. Student enjoys reading. _____

18. Student uses spelling patterns to assist with meaning. _____

19. Student enjoys reading aloud to the class. _____

20. Student reads at a higher level than what is expected at this grade level. _____

Comments: _____

_____

Checklist for Identifying Gifted Readers

Teacher Directions: *Use this checklist to help identify students who possess these characteristics. This form may also be placed in reading folders and sent to next year's teacher. [Adapted from Richards (2002) and Halsted (2002).]*

Name:	Date:	Teacher:

	Always	Sometimes	Never
1. Student reads above grade level	_____	_____	_____
2. Student reads longer than others in class.	_____	_____	_____
3. Student learns material faster.	_____	_____	_____
4. Student thinks strategically and revises strategies.	_____	_____	_____
5. Student displays self-confidence when reading.	_____	_____	_____
6. Student uses more than one strategy when creating meaning.	_____	_____	_____
7. Student looks at books to help solve problems.	_____	_____	_____
8. Student relates literature to his/her own life.	_____	_____	_____
9. Student is persistent and goal-oriented.	_____	_____	_____
10. Student thinks in abstract terms.	_____	_____	_____
11. Student mastered basic reading skills early in life.	_____	_____	_____
12. Student wants to talk in depth about books read.	_____	_____	_____
13. Student enjoys reading a variety of genres.	_____	_____	_____
14. Student comprehends material read.	_____	_____	_____
15. Student wants more time to read in class.	_____	_____	_____

Comments: _____

_____

After using one or both checklists, you will know which students in your classroom may need advanced reading instruction. The next question is this: Does the basal text provide appropriate learning and challenge for my gifted readers?

Rethinking the Basal Text

Many classroom reading programs rely on a basal text as a way for students to gain reading skills. Students are asked to read a story from their reading books, then answer questions at the end of the story that help teachers measure their comprehension. Additional activities are often suggested to help students think about the story. Gifted readers need instruction in reading that is different from that offered in a regular classroom (Collins & Aiex, 1995).

VanTassel-Baska (1998) states that the traditional use of a basal reading series typically focuses too much time and attention on mastering the reading process— particularly phonics, which gifted students don't need—rather than encouraging advanced students to interact with good literature.

Can the basal text be considered the "stand-alone" unit of reading instruction for gifted readers? The answer is NO—not if we plan to attend to the needs of our gifted readers.

Trade Books in the Classroom

Most gifted readers are ready to reach far beyond the basic skills offered in basal text reading programs. Because trade books are not limited by being written for specific grade levels—as basals are—the use of trade books can help gifted children connect with innumerable topics at whatever level of reading they enjoy.

Trade books are books of various sizes that can be found in libraries, bookstores, and on bookshelves in classrooms. They can be long or short, fiction or nonfiction, paper or hardback. They cover diverse subjects at virtually every reading level.

The use of trade books in reading programs is beneficial to all students, not just gifted readers. Trade books introduce students to a wide variety of subjects and thinking skills, including creative and critical thinking. Whereas selections in a basal reader are typically very short, trade books give students permission to "get lost in a good storyline," creating a learning environment that is inclusive for all students. Integrating trade books within reading programs helps to foster higher-level learning among gifted readers. Although the focus of this book is on gifted readers, the activities and strategies presented here can be adapted for use with all learners.

In the same way that specific titles are recommended for students who may be struggling in reading, *Literature Links* contains certain titles that have been recommended by experts in the field of gifted education. For more information on why certain titles have been selected, readers can refer to Judith Halsted's book *Some of My Best Friends Are Books, 2nd Edition* (2002). A former librarian and gifted program coordinator who led book discussion groups with gifted children, Halsted emphasizes that children grow intellectually as well as socially and emotionally through reading good books. She also discusses the role of books in bibliotherapy and as aids to better self-esteem. Her book, an annotated bibliography, contains many recommendations for gifted readers K-12 and includes plot summaries, questions for discussion, themes, and reading levels. The index of themes is particularly helpful.

Whereas *Some of My Best Friends Are Books* (Halsted, 2002) contains short summaries of nearly 300 books, *Literature Links* contains extended classroom activities for 10 of the books recommended by Halsted. The activities are designed to help teachers fold these books into their curriculum. Activities require students to use higher-level thinking and to be self-directed in creating projects. They expose students to different cultures and advanced vocabulary. When teachers use these activities with their advanced readers, they will not only bring challenge and motivation to their gifted students, they will also be encouraged to design similar activities for other trade books that they may bring to their classrooms—a winning solution for all.

Key Points

- Gifted readers display strong skills, deep understanding, and a passion for learning through the written word.

- Without opportunities for interesting and challenging literature choices, gifted readers may become disruptive or inattentive.

- Gifted readers may not be advanced in other cognitive areas.

- Tools to identify gifted readers are suggested or included.

- Trade books from the library, local booksellers, or tucked away on classroom shelves may be best choices for gifted readers.

Chapter 2
Using Trade Books with Gifted Readers

Many bright and gifted people suppress awareness of their need to learn. Teaching these children to use books is one way of demonstrating that learning is important to them and that books can be a significant part of their lives.

—Judith Wynn Halsted

The Teacher's Role

Literature and trade books are highly valuable for gifted readers for several reasons. While all children benefit from the integration of trade books into their reading instruction, certain titles are particularly effective with students who are gifted. The teacher's role is to choose appropriate books for the students. The following discussion points will help educators understand why the use of trade books with gifted readers is so important and powerful.

Why Gifted Readers Need Trade Books

Many experts in gifted education and reading instruction have written about the value of literature for gifted readers. Judith Halsted (1990) established the need for using trade books in the classroom when she stated, "teachers working with groups of children can promote intellectual as well as social and emotional development by using literature as a supplement to reading basal texts" (p. 2). Teachers can encourage discussion and foster higher-level learning with gifted readers as they integrate appropriately selected trade books into their classrooms.

Imagine walking into a classroom and watching students read stories and novels with enthusiasm. Imagine for a moment what classrooms would be like if the shelves were full of quality literature enticing students to read daily. Think of the excitement of visiting classes that regularly hold literature discussion groups!

Educators know that advanced readers are typically more involved and more interested in reading. They frequently read for interest, enjoyment, and learning (Richards,

2002). The use of trade books not only engages readers in new knowledge, but it helps them identify characters who have needs that are similar to their own. The ideal classroom provides gifted readers with time to browse and select books to read, as well as time to discuss the books that they have read. But how many of us have the time and resources to manage an "ideal classroom"? Not many. However, the goal of engaging readers in new knowledge *can* be accomplished with the help of the school librarian and trade books.

Using trade books in the classroom helps students maintain a positive relationship with reading. Teachers who integrate the use of trade books with gifted readers accomplish many things:

➤ Literature allows students to enjoy stories and to be exposed to rich vocabulary.

➤ Trade books help students to explore new topics and to generate new ideas.

➤ Students who experience a variety and balance of reading material build creative, critical, and imaginative thinking skills.

➤ Students who read widely begin to appreciate their own cultures as they learn about others.

➤ Advanced readers who are exposed to trade books will appreciate other points of view.

➤ Gifted students who read trade books will grow intellectually, as well as in their social and emotional development.

➤ Trade books can help proficient students take some control of their own learning.

I love to read! I wish we had more time during school to read on our own. Reading takes me to far away places.
                                        —fourth-grade gifted reader

The Importance of Using Trade Books

Use the illustration below to help you understand the importance of using trade books with gifted readers.

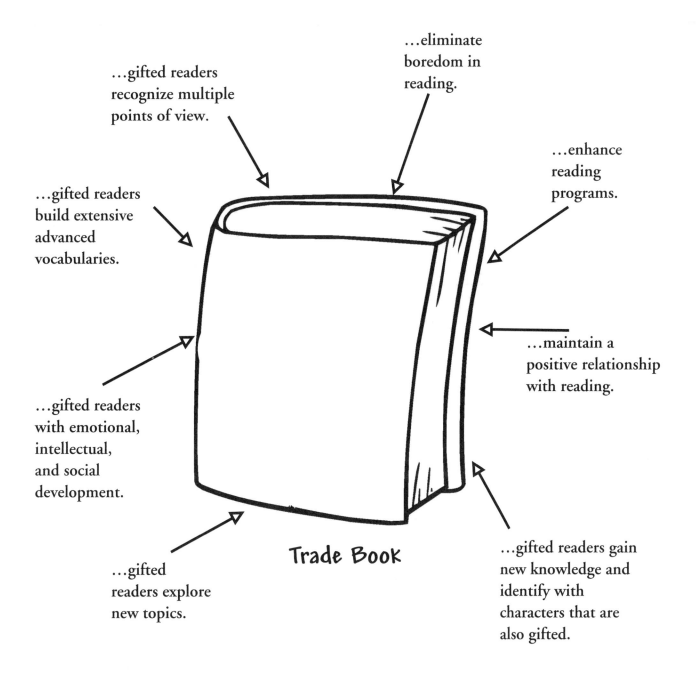

…gifted readers recognize multiple points of view.

…eliminate boredom in reading.

…enhance reading programs.

…gifted readers build extensive advanced vocabularies.

…gifted readers with emotional, intellectual, and social development.

…maintain a positive relationship with reading.

…gifted readers explore new topics.

Trade Book

…gifted readers gain new knowledge and identify with characters that are also gifted.

Teachers who wish to develop reading programs that meet the needs of gifted readers should begin by incorporating the use of trade books into their classrooms. There are easy ways for teachers who make the decision to integrate various literary titles to select appropriate and effective books for gifted readers.

Selecting Trade Books for Gifted Readers

How do you know which books to use? Several experts in the field of gifted education have published annotated lists or bibliographies containing excellent titles for gifted readers. Teachers can use bibliographies by Halsted (2002), Kingore (2001; 2002b), and Reis, Gubbins, and Richards (2002) to save time and to take advantage of what has already been proven to work well with bright students in the classroom. Rogers (2002a) also has a short list of titles recommended for gifted readers (which is located in Table 9.7) in her book *Re-Forming Gifted Education: How Parents and Teachers Can Match the Program to the Child*. She also lists inspiring biographical and autobiographical selections for gifted children (Table 9.6) and sources for finding good children's books (Table 9.10).

Andrea Butler and Jan Turbil have written a resource for teachers and parents titled *Towards a Reading and Writing Classroom* (1987). They not only provide information about the reading and writing process, they also offer instructional strategies to promote reading for all students. Butler and Turbil stress the importance of immersing children in good literature, as well as making wise decisions when selecting books: "The stories teachers read need to be chosen carefully. It is not good enough to grab a book from the library shelf without thinking about what is to be read and why it is to be read to the children" (p. 47). They add that appropriate selection can help teachers and students address issues such as racism and the plight of the disabled. Teachers are the link between students' interests and the books that will help them find the answers to questions that they might have.

How to Select Trade Books

Choosing books to provide for the intellectual and emotional needs of the gifted reader and helping children to select their own reading require some careful thought (Halsted, 2002). Teachers and librarians should consider the following criteria when selecting literature for gifted readers (Soltan, 2002):

> ➤ Language should be rich, varied, precise, complex, and exciting.
> ➤ Stories should be open-ended and inspire contemplative behavior.
> ➤ Books should leave the reader with as many questions as answers.
> ➤ Fiction should be complex enough to allow interpretive and evaluative behavior.
> ➤ Non-fiction should help students build problem-solving skills and develop methods of productive thinking.

Teachers should also consider titles that feature characters who are bright and talented, creative, "different," idealists, perfectionists, or unusually emotionally sensitive. These are traits inherent in many gifted children, and high-ability students need opportunities to identify with the main characters in the literature they read.

Research and Selection Process

Teachers should try to anticipate the needs of their gifted readers before these needs become problems (Halsted, 2002). The goal is to help students move through life's unpredictable stages by providing information about what they might expect, with examples of how others have dealt with similar challenges. Books provide these examples. Selections should portray characters who are intelligent, talented, resourceful, and/or inventive within a well-developed plot sequence, because this will be more intriguing to a gifted child. Biographies of individuals with the same or similar interests—who were considered gifted or talented both before and during the time of their public accomplishments—are an excellent choice for student reading (Soltan, 2002).

Gifted readers tend to have certain common behavioral characteristics that affect their reading needs. For example, gifted learners are often quite emotionally sensitive. To help children who have a need for understanding sensitivity—one's own and others— Halsted (2002) recommends *The View from Saturday* by E. L. Konigsburg and *The Bat Poet* by Randall Jarrell. Another example of a common characteristic of gifted learners is perfectionism. Some gifted children try to be perfect to the point of causing themselves physical symptoms such as headaches and stomachaches. For these children, *Don't Feed the Monster on Tuesdays* by Adolph Moser is a good choice (Halsted, 2002).

Gifted readers often feel alone or different from their age peers. These feelings can lead to frustration, poor self-esteem, or difficulty finding friends. Teachers may be able to help children avoid negative feelings by providing quality literature that helps them cope with feelings of differentness. *Archibald Frisby* by Michael Chesney will help gifted students in younger grades cope with the issue of being different (Halsted, 2002).

My teacher told me that I couldn't read a novel during class because it's a novel I'll be reading in class next year. That makes me so upset! I would like to read novels and stories that I'm interested in this year and not wait until next year. This just doesn't seem fair.
                                                    —fourth-grade student

Teacher Questionnaire for Selecting Books for Gifted Readers

Note to Teachers: Reproduce this page and place it in a "Selecting Books" folder. Fill out the forms as you find books that are appropriate for your readers. Use them as resources throughout the year. (Adapted from Reis, Gubbins, & Richards, 2002.)

Title of Book:_____Author:_____

Date Reviewed: _____Teacher:_____

Ask yourself:

1. What is my purpose for selecting the book?

2. Does the book provide a base for intriguing interaction?

3. Are there several elements that encourage high-order thinking?

4. Does the book offer solutions to conflicts?

5. Does the book leave the reader with questions or possibilities to evaluate decisions made by the characters?

6. Is there an event or situation that is appealing to the intellectually curious?

7. Does the book introduce skills? Is it based on a theme?

8. Are there gifted characters in the story?

9. Is there something in the book that will open new doors for gifted readers?

10. Is the content appropriate for my students?

11. Why would my students be interested in reading this book?

Additional comments about the book: _____

_____

The Book "Selectilizer"

Note to Teachers: Although teachers should not always be expected to complete checklists and forms before choosing books for gifted readers, this "selectilizer" will help you look for specific elements in literature. Teachers may want to use this tool until it becomes easier to locate specific titles.

Title of Book:_____Author:_____
Date Reviewed: _____Teacher:_____

1. Is the language rich, complex, and exciting?

2. Is the story open-ended? Does it provide questions that allow for higher-level thinking?

3. Does the book help students solve problems and develop methods of productive thinking?

4. Does the book allow readers to learn about relationships with others?

5. Is the readability appropriate?

6. Do the illustrations help reflect and enhance the plot?

7. Do the characters learn to accept someone who is different?

8. Do the characters struggle with issues such as moral courage or ethical choices?

9. Does the book provide humor?

10. Does the book depict characters who may face identity problems?

11. Do you feel that your students will enjoy this book?

12. Can differentiated instruction be integrated with the use of this book?

13. Will this book allow its readers to learn about different cultures and diverse populations?

Additional comments about the book: _____

_____

Key Points

✎ Literature helps students explore new topics and generate new ideas.

✎ Appropriately selected trade books promote emotional as well as intellectual development.

✎ Gifted readers who read trade books identify with characters and recognize multiple points of view.

✎ Trade books help gifted readers build their vocabularies.

✎ Books for gifted readers should promote higher-level thinking

✎ Books for gifted readers should include elements that offer solutions to conflicts.

✎ Books for gifted readers should contain characters with gifted traits.

Chapter 3
Differentiated Strategies for Gifted Readers

Books for the gifted need to be assessed not only in terms of language, structure, and content, but also by their potential for eliciting intellectual responses from the readers.

—Barbara Baskin and Karen Harris

This chapter will help teachers to establish differentiated reading programs in their classrooms. It defines "differentiation of instruction" and provides ideas and steps necessary to begin the process of differentiation. The teacher will understand what a differentiated classroom looks like and how to begin. Each of the strategies can be easily adapted for use with all students.

Examining Your Current Reading Program

To begin, teachers need to review and examine carefully their current reading programs and then ask themselves this question: What specific skills and areas need to be presented to all students? For example, all students must meet basic standards and criteria established by local school districts. Focusing on skills that must be acquired by all students provides a foundation for subsequent differentiated instruction that can avoid learning gaps.

Teachers can begin examining their reading programs by looking at student progress. They can look at each students' standardized test scores, rubrics, writing samples, anecdotal records, portfolios, running records, and task activity sheets. Data collected from these various evaluation tools is then analyzed and applied to the task of designing a differentiated classroom that incorporates instructional strategies that meet the needs of gifted readers. If standardized test scores show that a child has a grade equivalency of three years beyond his or her present grade, then the teacher knows that the child needs more advanced books with more challenging vocabulary and content. If writing samples show advanced language usage, the child needs to be reading material with more challenging concepts and language.

What Is a Differentiated Classroom?

Carol Tomlinson, a specialist in curriculum for gifted students, writes that differentiated classrooms are places where the needs of all learners are met—where both slow learners and rapid learners are given appropriate work and instruction. She urges teachers to assume that different learners have different needs, and she asks them to be proactive in meeting those needs: "In a differentiated classroom, commonalities are acknowledged and built upon, and student differences become important elements in teaching and learning as well" (2001, p.1).

According to Tomlinson (2001), differentiation:

➤ is "shaking up" what goes on in the classroom so that students have multiple options for taking in information.

➤ is a blend of whole-class, group, and individual instruction.

➤ "provides multiple approaches to content, process, and product."

Other experts have given generally similar descriptions, though they sometimes have a slightly different emphasis. Diane Heacox, author of *Differentiating Instruction in the Regular Classroom* (2002), says that differentiation means:

➤ recognizing the learning diversity represented in today's classrooms.

➤ acknowledging what students already know and can do.

➤ using flexible instructional grouping to provide opportunities for students to learn with others who have similar needs, styles, or preferences (p. 17).

Susan Winebrenner, author of *Teaching Gifted Kids in the Regular Classroom* (2001), states that differentiation provides gifted students with:

➤ different tasks and activities than their peers.

➤ tasks that lead to real learning.

➤ consistent opportunities to enjoy learning and to be as challenged and productive as possible (p. 5).

According to Carol Strip and Gretchen Hirsch, authors of *Helping Gifted Children Soar* (2000), "differentiation for gifted students means providing learning options that meet students' special needs for acceleration of content and greater depth, breadth and complexity of instruction" (p. 71).

Differentiation for Gifted Students

Differentiating curriculum for gifted students means providing experiences for all students to excel through a variety of instructional experiences and strategies. It becomes crucial for educators to manipulate the curriculum in ways that allow for academic growth to be achieved by the gifted students, as well as by average students.

By now, you are probably thinking, "How can I do all that while still meeting all of the other curriculum requirements?" While everyone agrees that beginning to differentiate instruction is time consuming, it does get easier as teachers and students learn how to work together. Strip and Hirsch helps us understand that differentiating instruction can be easier than we think: "It's actually easy to engage gifted children because they are open to so many different approaches and are excited about opportunities to accelerate or expand their learning in certain interest areas" (2000, p. 72).

In a differentiated classroom, instruction is student-centered, and flexible grouping is used. It is important to note that differentiated instruction should be qualitatively different instead of just quantitatively different, meaning that gifted students should not be given simply more of the same work that they may already have mastered (Tomlinson, 1995).

Differentiating Reading Instruction for Gifted Readers

Remember the anxiety you had as a teacher during the first week of school when you realized that your third-grade classroom contained some students reading on the second-grade level and others reading at the sixth-grade level? At that point, you had to make a decision to either follow the basal reading text and keep everyone on the same level (and in the same material) or to find other books and activities to meet the needs of all of students in the class. Even though it is sometimes difficult and frustrating, the choice must be to find those more challenging materials. "The lack of challenging materials is one factor that discourages the continued reading development of advanced readers" (Kingore, 2002a, p. 2).

Keeping this in mind, the first step to providing challenge for gifted readers is to understand that assessment must be ongoing in order to have accurate knowledge of students' actual ability levels. Knowing the reading levels of your advanced readers is critical to finding appropriate trade books and designing suitable instructional strategies. For example, that third-grade girl who is reading at a sixth-grade level (as shown in standardized achievement test grade equivalency scores) will need reading material that approximates or is somewhat higher than a sixth-grade reading level.

The following information about differentiation will help you provide challenge for your gifted readers through a variety of strategies. Most are easy to implement, and some can be used with all students, not just with gifted students.

Ways to Differentiate Instruction

Learning Contracts

In this strategy, as gifted readers demonstrate mastery in specific skills areas, they can develop different types of learning contracts in partnership with their teachers. These contracts become bonding documents that note certain activities which gifted readers will complete while other students work on assigned projects. Contracts give gifted readers opportunities to practice skills—to read, discuss, analyze, and write—with literature they find interesting and challenging. Learning contracts can include assignments, extension activities, timelines, and rules that students must follow as they complete their contracts. Both student and teacher sign and date the contract to show that they are in agreement as to its requirements.

Gifted readers usually enjoy contracts because they can take ownership and be in charge to some extent of their own learning. Examples of learning contracts are offered in the Appendix, as well as in Winebrenner's *Teaching Gifted Kids in the Regular Classroom* (2001).

19

Permission to Read Ahead

This simple strategy, noted by Susan Winebrenner (2001), gives rapid readers a "contract for permission to read ahead." This strategy allows advanced readers to remain challenged and motivated by reading ahead at a pace that is more comfortable for them. Both teacher and student sign an actual written contract, with the student agreeing not to divulge the story's ending to the others in the class. The contract also describes the activities that the student will engage in while the rest of the class finishes the book.

Curriculum Compacting

This is a strategy to be used whenever you discover that some of your students have already learned part or all of the curriculum that you are about to teach. When you find that certain students have already mastered certain material, you allow them to skip the regular work in order to move forward by reading a different literature selection.

Curriculum compacting can be used to make adjustments for students in any curriculum area at any grade level. Winebrenner helps us understand this strategy by stating, "we need to determine what competencies certain students already have and give them full credit for what they already know" (2001, p. 32). She offers five steps to help us get started using curriculum compacting in our classrooms:

1. Identify the learning objectives or standards that all students must learn.

2. Offer a pre-test opportunity to those students who think they have already mastered the content.

3. Plan and offer curriculum extensions for those students who are successful with the compacting opportunities.

4. Eliminate all drill, practice, and review for state or standardized tests for students who have already mastered such things.

5. Keep accurate records (p. 32).

Teachers who use curriculum compacting in reading should begin by administering a pre-test, which can be given informally, orally, or in writing from the basal text series. Students who show mastery by scoring 85% or better on the pre-test will do replacement (other) activities for that part of the curriculum. The replacement or alternative assignment might allow the gifted readers to read books which they select themselves or to complete other teacher-assigned reading. Students will all be reading at the same time; however, the advanced readers will be reading material that better matches their particular abilities, skills, needs, and interests.

Winebrenner further explains the process of compacting by using the words "trash" and "garbage." Parts of the curriculum represent "trash" or "garbage" to gifted readers because they don't need to learn it. They already know it; they can throw it away and not worry about it.

Another analogy is that of buying back time. Once gifted readers demonstrate knowledge and mastery of certain "chunks" or pieces of the curriculum, they are allowed to essentially "buy back" that time and spend it working on other learning. Gifted students should never be required to "waste time" by sitting through something they already know or can do.

Questioning

Questioning is an important strategy to use with gifted readers for many different reasons. We already know that gifted readers learn at a faster pace than their peers and should be exposed to information that adds to their knowledge base. Part of this process involves teaching gifted readers to pose their own questions, as well as to respond to higher-level questions posed by others.

Questioning enables teachers and students to establish what is already known, to use and extend this knowledge, and then to develop new ideas (Painter, 1996). Using higher-level questioning with gifted readers increases students' awareness, fosters logical thinking, and promotes decision making. Questioning is a critical strategy that helps gifted readers get the most out of literature.

Benefits of Questioning

Jo Painter (1996) cites the following benefits of questioning with gifted students:

> ➤ It provides a structure to examine ideas and information.
> ➤ It is integral to developing reflective and metacognitive thinking (or in other words, thinking about one's own thinking).
> ➤ It requires students and teachers to reflect on their understandings and can lead to changes and improvements in learning, thinking, and teaching.

Questioning remains one of the most effective instructional tools in classrooms. It can be easily implemented, requires few or no supplies, and provides teachers with useful and credible data. Most educators understand the benefit of questioning. Their only question is: How do we implement this strategy so that it is effective in our classrooms?

Guidelines for Questioning

Teachers should first examine the questions found in the basal reading text. These questions can be a guide to ensure that gifted readers are learning and maintaining the skills needed to meet the "benchmarks" or standards on standardized tests as established by most school districts.

Beyond questions in the basal text, the kinds of questions that teachers ask are important. Far too many questions asked in classrooms today require only a simple *yes* or *no* response. These are called "closed-ended questions" because they require only a one-word answer and little or no thought. They are knowledge-level questions only and give students the mistaken idea that all learning is fact-based, with one right answer—*yes* or *no*. The world is a complicated place with problems that don't necessarily have one right answer, and students should be taught to think beyond that. With this in mind, reading teachers should use more open-ended, complex questions that require students to analyze and evaluate situations or the characters' actions and decisions. All students need to have practice responding to higher-level questions. Gifted students in particular, with their love of argument, debate, and analysis, particularly need experience responding to higher-level questions.

The following information will help teachers generate and use more open-ended questions with gifted readers.

Types of Questions for Gifted Readers

All learners should have experience with many different types of questions. However, gifted learners and gifted readers need to practice the higher levels of thinking and questioning more of the time. They are able to think at these levels, but they need practice and guidance to develop their skills. Bloom's Taxonomy of Thinking is helpful when teachers begin to develop questions that require thinking. This Taxonomy (1956) is an organized structure of thinking that progresses from lower to higher levels of complexity.

The elements of Bloom's Taxonomy can help teachers construct effective questions for gifted readers.

Knowledge: Recalls facts and terms.

Comprehension: Demonstrates understanding by explaining or organizing.

Application: Solves problems by applying new information.

Analysis: Examines and breaks apart information to look at it in a new way.

Synthesis: Puts ideas or parts together to form a new whole.

Evaluation: Defends one's opinions or makes judgments based on criteria.

Teachers can meet all students' needs by varying the levels of questions. Questions at lower levels—"knowledge" and "comprehension"—help determine what children already know and understand. For example, "What is an earthquake?" is a knowledge-level question. "What happens in an earthquake?" is a comprehension question.

Application questions can be used with virtually all students. For example, "How would you use your knowledge of earthquakes to design a safer building?" is an application question.

Questions at the "analysis" level encourage students to think more creatively and critically. The question "Why or how is an earthquake similar to a tsunami?" is an analysis question. It requires students to think about what they know and take elements from one field of knowledge and apply them to another, or to take apart an idea to look at its parts more closely.

Questions at the "synthesis" and "evaluation" levels are the most challenging and are the questions that gifted students seem to enjoy most. A synthesis question would be: "Explain why predicting earthquakes and tsunamis is difficult." To respond, students must take information about earthquakes, and then take information about tsunamis, and with reasoning, put the information together to give the best answer they can. An example of an evaluation question would be: "In your opinion, what do scientists and others need to do to protect citizens from earthquakes and tsunamis in the future?" To answer this question, students must again review and examine the information they have about tsunamis and earthquakes and come up with their own thoughts about how government and science might protect citizens in the future. Evaluation requires open-ended thinking based on prior knowledge, and students should be asked to give support for their reasoning.

There is no one right answer in any of the higher-level thinking questions. Students who work with higher-level thinking will learn that there can be several points of view with several different reasons behind those points of view. With more experience in critical thinking, students learn to apply criteria to those solutions and gain competency in evaluating solutions.

For another way to understand how Bloom's levels of thinking can help teachers formulate questions for the classroom, read the following example. Remember that gifted students need plenty of questions that require them to think at the three highest levels—analysis, synthesis, and evaluation.

Level 1: Knowledge
What is _____?
How did _____ happen?
Which character _____?
Who was _____?
In what year did _____ occur?

Level 2: Comprehension
How would you restate the meaning of _____?
What can you say about _____ (character) from the story?
How would you summarize Chapter 3 from the story? _____
Where does the story take place? _____

Level 3: Application
How would you use _____?
How could you tell a friend about _____?
What examples can you find that the character _____?

Level 4: Analysis
What is the theme of the story? _____
What motive(s) did (character) have? _____
What clues do we have that _____?
Why and how did (character) change? _____

Level 5: Synthesis
What changes would you make to help solve _____?
How would you improve the story? _____
Can you invent a new _____?
How would you best describe_____?

Level 6: Evaluation
If you were the author, are there any parts in the story that you would change? _____
Why or why not? _____
Would you recommend this book to a friend? _____
Why or why not? _____
Why do you think the author chose to write this story? _____

Using Questioning with Gifted Readers

There are several ways in which teachers can implement questioning strategies with their students. One way is to assign gifted readers to read a trade book independently. Then provide time for these students to participate in literature discussion groups where they can discuss and answer questions with the teacher. Another way is to give each reader a folder containing open-ended, high-order questions. After reading a trade book, the student answers the questions in the folder and returns it to the teacher for assessment purposes. The questions can be tailored to the student.

Still another way to implement questioning is for the teacher to read an appropriately selected trade book aloud to *all students* in the class. After reading the book, students are given time for reflection by answering questions developed by the teacher. Students that need reinforcement in areas such as comprehension and application will be given folders containing these types of questions. Gifted readers will receive folders that contain questions based on Bloom's higher levels—analysis, synthesis, and evaluation.

All students should be given opportunities to reach higher levels of learning through the use of appropriately developed questions, but this must be accomplished when each student is ready to accomplish such tasks.

Literature Discussion Groups

Judith Halsted (2002) suggests holding discussion groups with students who have read the same book and are generally around the same age. During these group discussions, gifted readers can debate issues and evaluate characters found in the story. Teachers often ask if this strategy can be used with students who are not considered gifted in reading. Absolutely! Group discussions are an excellent way to reach all learners, regardless of ability levels. The procedure for holding successful discussion groups follows:

1. Literature discussion groups are formed based on student abilities and books read. Gifted readers are grouped together. Average readers are grouped together. Slow readers are grouped together. The teacher chooses an appropriate book for each group.

2. The teacher makes sure that all students understand the rules for participating in literature discussion groups.

3. Each student reads the assigned book independently and at scheduled times during the day.

4. Discussion groups take place two or three times a week, depending upon the length of the books. The teacher determines the length of time that is spent in each group.

5. The teacher establishes general focus areas for the literature discussion groups as follows:
   — Character analysis
   — Setting, plot, and sequence
   — Dialogue between characters
   — Identifying conflict and solutions and evaluating these
   — Questions focusing on open-ended responses

6. The teacher offers a variety of ways for students to share their information. Students may choose to record their responses on tape, write their answers on paper, or lead a discussion and then complete a reflection form to ensure that all students participate.

7. The teacher will monitor and evaluate each group for effectiveness. He or she will look for participation among group members, the group's ability to stay on task, each student's ability to ask appropriate questions, the group's ability to debate in a positive manner, and each student's ability to demonstrate knowledge of the book read.

The key to success with this strategy with gifted readers is the grouping. Gifted readers should be grouped together in such a way that they can feel safe in verbalizing and sharing their insights. Students who are grouped by abilities for reading instruction have been found to have increased understanding and appreciation for literature (Sakiey, 1980).

Journals

Having students respond to their reading in journals helps them reflect on given stories, examine their own thinking, make predictions, and express their thoughts and feelings in writing. Journals can be simple notebooks purchased at local office supply stores, or they can be created by the teacher or student. They may be for unspecified responses or to meet specific instructional goals. Teachers may read the journals and may even write comments to respond to the child, but they typically do not grade the journals, since that could discourage free writing of ideas. This dialog journal becomes a two-way communication between teacher and child and lets the teacher know if the child is experiencing any difficulties. Descriptions of several types of journals follow.

Free-Write Journal

A free-write journal is a place where students can feel free to write about many different things—the day's events or problems, or a response to a question provided by the teacher. Free-write journals can also be used with partners. Students can write to a journal buddy, and the buddy can respond. It is an easy way to get students writing and thinking using their written communication skills.

Reflective and Response Journals

These types of journals, as they relate to literature, are used to encourage gifted readers to record their thoughts and feelings about a story's events or the actions of certain characters. In *Old Turtle,* by Douglas Wood, the turtle announces the coming of human beings to the earth. Students reading this story might respond in their journals by recording their thoughts about this announcement and how the animals might have felt about it. Response/reflective journals give gifted readers opportunities to use some of the higher-level thinking skills—analysis, synthesis, and evaluation. Some questions that students might address in a reflective response journal are:

➤ What happened?
➤ How did I feel?
➤ What did I learn?

Multiple Entry Journal

This journal gives gifted readers opportunities to respond to text as they read, making entries whenever they choose. Whereas in reflective/response journals, students record information learned, in the multiple entry journal, students focus on their individual thoughts about characters and their actions. They may write to answer the questions:

➤ What character in the book captured your interest?

➤ What detail about this character was of particular interest to you?

➤ How did this character make you feel?

Illustration Journal

This journal is an excellent tool to use with gifted readers at younger grade levels. It allows students to read a book and respond by either writing or drawing an illustration.

➤ Describe the events of the story in the order they occurred.

➤ Create a strip story illustrating the important events of the story in the order they occurred.

Critical Thinking Journal

This journal is simply a place where gifted readers respond to questions developed by teachers. The questions should be based on Bloom's Taxonomy of Thinking. Teachers may develop questions about the story and place a copy of these questions in the students' journals. Or the teacher may choose to give gifted readers one or two questions at a time. Different students can respond to different questions. The advantage of this strategy is that teachers have great flexibility with individual students as they encourage critical thinking through the use of journals.

Synthesis Journal

A synthesis journal allows students opportunities to examine information to see how it relates to the whole picture. Students can then apply new information to their own personal lives and determine how they might want to use this new knowledge or information.

➤ What new information did you learn from this story?

➤ How might you use this information in another class or outside of school?

Quotation Journal

The use of this type of journal promotes the development of critical reading. It encourages students to reflect on quotations found within a story by asking questions on how the quotations affect the story.

➤ What quotation from the book captured your interest?

➤ How did this quotation make you feel?

➤ Why is this quotation important to the story?

Comprehensive Journal

This type of journal is for all teachers who like to keep everything neat and tidy and in one area. This journal can be labeled with tabs on separate sections for easy access. Sections in comprehensive journals might include facts and information, thoughts and opinions, new vocabulary, and notes.

Prediction Journal

This type of journal is particularly helpful when gifted readers are in the process of reading an assigned book. Students will stop at different points in the story and make predictions about upcoming events. Identify the place in the story where the students should stop and make their predictions. Include a description of the action and the page number. Students may also decide to stop at other points in the story and make predictions from there about what will happen next.

> ➤ What do you predict will happen next?
> ➤ After you have finished reading, return to the relevant page and record what actually happened.

Guidelines for Journal Use

1. Make journals ahead of time using small notebooks, stapled paper, or student-created booklets. Decide which type of journal best fits the needs of your advanced readers.

2. Model ways to use journals to ensure that students learn to date every entry and write more than one sentence. Put a sample journal entry up on an overhead transparency or *PowerPoint*® slide.

3. Establish a regular time during reading instruction for students to respond in their journals.

4. Create criteria for evaluation of journal entries. Ask for student input.

5. Keep your own journal to model for students the importance of thinking, writing, reflecting, and recording thoughts.

6. Integrate the use of journals into other subject areas.

7. Allow students time to share favorite journal entries with the class.

Flexible Grouping

In this strategy, teachers meet individual needs by informally grouping and re-grouping students in a variety of ways (Valentino, 2000). Flexible grouping means placing students in different groups at different times based on student readiness and/or interests. Gifted readers benefit from working in groups with peers who are able to work at the same ability level. Flexible grouping is an excellent way to meet the needs of gifted readers, as well as to differentiate instruction.

Catherine Valentino (2000) helps us understand the importance of implementing different grouping strategies in classrooms. Teachers who divide students into groups based on individual needs have the flexibility to offer individualized instruction. While the groups are completing given tasks, teachers can work one-on-one with gifted readers. And gifted readers have the chance to work on reading projects and strategies that meet their advanced needs.

Valentino says, "teachers who use flexible grouping strategies often employ several organizational patterns for instruction" (2000, p. 1). She describes two organizational patterns.

Teacher-Led Groups

This grouping strategy is a good way to introduce a new topic or theme, conclude a lesson or unit, meet with small groups of students, and/or provide individual instruction when needed. Examples of teacher-led groups are whole class instruction, small group instruction, and students working alone on individualized teacher-generated activities.

Student-Led Groups

Student groups can take many forms, but they all share a common feature—students control the group dynamics. Some examples of student-led groups follow.

Collaborative or cooperative groups: Students share ideas and learn together as they solve a problem or complete an assignment.

Circle sharing:	One student gives the group an open-ended question, statement, or problem. Other students take turns responding with solutions. Student leaders rotate.
Four corners:	The teacher poses a question or problem that has four parts. Students choose which part they want to help solve and then move to a designated part of the room indicated as the "solving corner" for that part of the question or problem. Students in each corner work together to solve that part of the problem and then reconvene with the rest of the class to share solutions.

Performance-based groups: Groups of students with like needs may be grouped together temporarily to gain access to a specific concept or skill.

Group study:	This strategy may be most effective following whole group instruction. After a concept or skill is discussed in class, the smaller group acts to reinforce, expand on, or test their skill or knowledge.
Interview for options:	After an individual learning activity, group members will interview one another to share and reinforce their learning.

Student dyads: Students are grouped in pairs, allowing for peer and cross-age instructional interaction.

Tiered Assignments

In this strategy, teachers provide assignments with varying levels of difficulty. Although all students will be studying the same general topic, some will work with basic concepts, while others will be working with information that represents greater breadth and depth. Some students will have materials at grade level, and others will have reading materials written at higher levels. Some students will have more work at the knowledge and comprehension levels, while others will have tasks incorporating the higher levels of thinking—analysis and synthesis. The goal is to provide challenge for all students.

Tomlinson (2001) describes tiered assignments as the "meat and potatoes" of differentiated instruction. Teachers can use tiered assignments to make sure that students explore "varied levels of activities that ensure that students explore ideas at a level that builds on their prior knowledge. When the task difficulty and skill level are slightly above student level, real learning occurs." (p. 101).

According to Tomlinson (2001), tiered assignments:

➤ allow students to begin learning where they are.
➤ allow students to work with appropriately challenging tasks.
➤ avoid assigning work to students that is too hard and produces anxiety.
➤ combine instruction and assessment.
➤ promote student success (p.101).

How to Use Tiered Assignments

Teachers should:

➤ plan for three tiers when using tiered assignments for most classrooms.
➤ identify goals and objectives that each tier (or group) will be responsible to complete.
➤ make student outcomes clear to all groups.
➤ use a variety of assessment tools to determine appropriate ability levels for tasks.
➤ assess continuously so that all students receive appropriate assignments.
➤ give directions to each group so that everyone is aware of assigned activities.

What Activities Can Be Tiered?

The following activities can be tiered:

➤ assignments given in class.
➤ whole group instruction followed by activities.
➤ homework.
➤ learning centers.
➤ science experiments.
➤ assessments.

As an example:

Group 1:   Read _____.

Answer questions.

Write a summary to be put in a class newsletter.

Group 2:   Read _____.

Create a new ending to the story by writing a paragraph which you will read aloud.

Group 3:   Read _____.

Write a one-page paper telling why you think the character....

Teacher Conferences

One-on-one student conferences with the teacher help differentiate instruction by keeping lines of communication open, which can lead to advanced learning in the classroom. Gifted readers may read a book independently, in a group setting, or with the teacher. (Whatever the case, the teacher will have already read the book.) The teacher then schedules conferences, often at times when other students are reading independently, to promote dialog between the gifted reader and the teacher. These times can be used in various ways—to read, skim, scan, predict outcomes, redefine and compose meaning, or analyze and evaluate decisions and actions made by characters in the book.

Teacher/student conferences also help to generate discussions based on higher levels of learning through questioning. In addition, they can provide teachers with data that can be used to assess students' understanding of themes, as well as their social and emotional growth and understanding.

Sample Questions for Teacher/Student Conferences

1. Why do you believe the author chose to name the main character as he/she did?

2. Do you relate to any of the characters in the story? Do they seem real to you?

3. Are there parts of the story you don't completely understand?

4. What do you believe to be the main conflict in the story?

5. So far, what is your reaction to the story? Why?

6. Is there anything in this story that relates to your own life? Explain.

7. Has the theme of this story changed any of your beliefs? Explain.

Key Points

- ✎ Review the basal series selected for your grade level to see if it includes challenging options for advanced readers.

- ✎ Examine the processes suggested for differentiating reading instruction. Select options appropriate for the advanced readers in your class.

- ✎ Practice using higher-level, open-ended questions with your students, especially the advanced readers.

- ✎ Investigate strategies suggested in this chapter; i.e., learning contracts, literature discussion groups, journals, modified grouping structures, and teacher conferences.

Chapter 4

More Ideas for Gifted Readers

*Research documents that students benefit from the activities and
discussions that accompany reading. Activities that follow reading
experiences are most effective when they engage a child's mind,
interests, and feelings.*

—Bertie Kingore

This chapter summarizes more instructional strategies that have been proven effective in reading programs for gifted readers. Barbara Clark, author of the seminal textbook *Growing Up Gifted* (1983, 2002), states that gifted students need educational programs that offer small group discussions, flexibility, respect for others' ideas, time for reflection, and the opportunity to compare communication and decision-making processes with academic peers. Strategies included in this chapter support Clark's recommendations.

Learning Centers

Learning centers, also known as interest centers, are collections of activities or materials that promote or reinforce particular knowledge or skills or that appeal to identified interests of students. Centers provide differentiated instruction by addressing specific student interests and abilities. Teachers should choose the types of centers and the materials for them that will best meet the needs of their students. Tomlinson (2001) says, "interest centers can provide enrichment for students who demonstrate mastery with required work, and can be a vehicle for providing these students with meaningful study when required assignments are completed" (p. 100). The key to success when using centers for differentiated reading instruction is to vary the complexity of the materials and activities according to the achievement levels and abilities of the students.

Teachers who use centers in their classrooms give a message to students that they are willing to individualize assignments according to student interests and abilities—i.e., they care about their students. Students appreciate working in centers because boredom is no longer an issue. They have choices for their work in the centers.

Tomlinson (2001) says interest centers:

➤ allow for student choice.

➤ satisfy student curiosity as they explore hows and whys.

➤ allow students to study topics not found in the regular curriculum.

➤ allow students to study a topic in greater breadth and depth.

➤ allow students to make connections between fields of study in school and real life (p. 100).

Using Centers with Gifted Readers

Teachers can start by completing these tasks:

➤ Administer interest inventories to help determine student interests (Kanevsky, 1999; Renzulli, 1977; Rogers 2002a).

➤ Gather materials that will tap into those interests.

➤ Determine additional purpose(s) for using centers, such as improving a skill or expanding science knowledge.

➤ Gather materials and activities that will meet the additional purpose(s) of the centers.

➤ Determine center topics: writing, science, art, math, reading, or a combination of all subjects.

➤ Be prepared to adjust or modify centers by manipulating the materials to match student readiness and ability.

➤ Always explain the process and classroom management policies to students.

— When are students permitted to work in centers?

— Are students able to pre-test out of certain lessons in reading and then work in centers?

— Will students work in pairs, teams, or independently?

— If students have questions while in the centers, what should they do?

➤ Have clear guidelines for evaluating work time and grading work completed in the centers.

— How will students document their work?

— How will students be held accountable for their work?

Using Centers for Literature

Suppose that the whole class is reading *Where Do You Think You're Going, Christopher Columbus* by Jean Fritz. As students complete given reading assignments for the day, they proceed to the centers. Gifted readers proceed to centers A or B. Other students may proceed to centers C or D or work on seatwork.

Center A:	Use books, articles, and other resources in the center to answer questions found on index cards about Christopher Columbus.
Center B:	Use the index cards provided to play vocabulary match-up using words about the Columbus voyage. Write a brief story describing a day as a sailor on one of Columbus' three ships.

Chapters 5 and 6 contain specific activities that may be used in learning centers. You may want to mark titles or activities that correspond with stories in your basal text. Using centers with gifted readers is an excellent way to promote advanced learning while still using a basal reading text.

Literature Binders

Literature binders contain carefully selected activities, questions, and vocabulary words that relate to a specific book or literary piece. Teachers like them because they help students stay organized throughout a novel study. Students enjoy them because they get opportunities to work independently as well as in groups. The everyday reading routine seems to become energized when students work within their literature binders. The format of activities included in this book has been designed for use with literature binders, although activities and discussion questions can easily be implemented in other instructional ways.

Using a thin, inexpensive binder allows teachers to differentiate reading instruction for gifted readers in an organized fashion. A well-organized literature binder usually contains the following sections:

➤ *Timeline or overview of the literature unit*: This includes the title and author of the book to be read, a timeframe for completion of activities, and a goal sheet to be completed by the student.

➤ *Literature discussion questions*: Choose questions for students' binders based on the individual needs of each student. Higher-level questions are appropriate for advanced, gifted readers and are designed to elicit thought-provoking responses. Questions can be:
— assigned to students based on ability levels.
— offered as a choice.
— completed in small groups.
— completed independently.

➤ *Vocabulary study*: This section includes a list of vocabulary words that are found in the story to be read. This section of the binder also contains vocabulary activities and games to help reinforce the terms found in the story.

➤ *Literature extension activities*: This section of the binder contains a list of activities that help students think more deeply about the book being read. The activities found here can be color-coded so that the teacher can assign specific activities to specific groups of students.

➤ *Teacher and student reflections*: This section contains blank pages, much like a journal. The teacher encourages the students to use this section to record their thoughts, feelings, and reactions to the story.

The questions, vocabulary, and activities that follow in Chapters 5 and 6 can all be reproduced and placed directly into literature binders. Each student should have his or her own binder. Upon completion, the pages are evaluated by the teacher, then taken out, stapled together, and sent home. The binder is then ready for the next exciting story or novel. If students are working in groups, the teacher may create a different binder for each group and allow the students to follow the same format, only in a group setting.

Role Playing

Teachers of gifted readers can review many reading skills by asking the students to participate in a variety of role-play situations. Students may choose to identify the conflict in a story and then perform a short skit to teach the class about the conflict. Have students predict how they think the conflict will be solved and include their prediction in the skit. Using role play with gifted readers promotes planning and organizational skills. Role play also allows gifted readers time to express themselves in creative ways.

Reading Buddies

For this strategy, pair two compatible gifted readers together so that they can act as reading buddies and conduct their own team meetings. During scheduled times, the two reading buddies read their books together, share their thoughts, devise a list of questions, make predictions, read passages together, research given topics, and discuss and analyze the meaning of certain quotes. In this strategy, the teacher acts as a facilitator or a sidelines coach while encouraging advanced readers to reflect and respond to the book being read.

Having a reading buddy can be fun and can encourage creativity. Gifted readers may choose to use team names, team logos, team songs, team colors, and more. This strategy can also be used with students at different grade levels. For example, if a student in third grade is reading on a fifth-grade level, you may want to work something out with the fifth-grade teacher so that the third-grade student has a fifth-grade reading buddy. There are many different ways to use reading buddies with advanced readers. Give it a try!

Classroom Reading Box

This is an activity in which a parent volunteer can help. Ask a parent to decorate a "reading box" to be kept in the classroom. As gifted students read certain books, they can ask questions or make comments on index cards and place those cards in the reading box. This strategy is appropriate for all learners; however, you will find that your advanced readers truly enjoy writing to express themselves. Teachers may also choose to write higher-level questions on cards that may help students better understand the story. These cards can be kept in a tray or envelope near the box. As gifted readers answer the questions, they place the cards and their answers in the reading box for the teacher or parent volunteer to read and respond to. If a book is being read by the entire class, the teacher could have classmates choose cards at the end of the day and read the responses to the class.

How is this differentiated instruction? The questions written on the cards are differentiated by ability levels as well as by interests. Although all students will be placing cards in the reading box, questions are based on their interests, or sometimes on the pre-selected stories they read that were chosen for their reading ability levels. In that case, advanced readers will be responding to questions that were selected to meet that student's reading level, vocabulary, interests, and other needs.

Activity Menus

Activity menus are forms that list a variety of activities that extend a unit of study for advanced students. Students get to choose which activities from the menu that they would like to do. Or students can make up their own activities and add them to the menu.

Howard Gardner's theory of multiple intelligences (1983) teaches us that students learn differently and should be given opportunities to enhance specific intelligences through the infusion of different curriculum areas. There are seven intelligences defined by Howard Gardner: mathematical, verbal, musical, visual/spatial, interpersonal, intrapersonal, and kinesthetic. Educators who choose to use activity menus with gifted readers should incorporate as many of the intelligences as possible into the menus. To do this, teachers should have on hand a variety of activities—some of which would be appropriate and enjoyable to a child who likes to learn with rhythm and music, others that would appeal to a child who likes art and visual/spatial learning, and still others that would interest a child who likes logic or mathematical approaches—until there are activities for each of the intelligences.

A wide variety of resources are available to teachers interested in incorporating multiple intelligences, or MI, into their curriculum. A comprehensive listing of MI resources can be found at www.newhorizons.org for those teachers who would like to learn more.

Creating Activity Menus

Susan Winebrenner (2001) explains how teachers can use reading activity menus to facilitate choice, as well as to provide gifted readers with opportunities to take ownership in their learning:

➤ Prepare a list of activities from which students may choose.
➤ Tell students that they may choose an activity to work on during designated times.
➤ Invite students to come up with their own ideas and projects. These should be discussed with the teacher.
➤ Have students record their work and progress in a daily log.

Example of a Reading Activity Menu

Student Directions: Choose three of the activities listed below to do in place of your regular assignments. You will work on these projects during times designated by your teacher. Record dates for which you work, as well as any notes about the projects selected.

Name:_____Date: _____Teacher:_____

Dates: **Activity:**

_____   Create a new ending to the story.

_____   Create a short scene with dialog for two characters in the story.

_____   Find two others who have read the story. Conduct an interview to find out what they liked and didn't like about the story.

_____   Create a puppet show to depict the story you read.

_____   Create a book for younger children that is similar to this story. Think about plot, setting, conflict, and so on.

You may also choose to create your own three activities to complete. Write your ideas below and share them with your teacher. Think about areas that interest you.

_____

_____

_____

Student Comments:_____

_____

Teacher Comments:_____

_____

Adapted from S. Winebrenner (2001), *Teaching Gifted Kids in the Regular Classroom.*

The use of activity menus with gifted readers has been proven effective in most reading programs in regular classrooms. Teachers appreciate the simplicity and flexibility associated with activity menus. Students will enjoy the "control" they receive from having choices as they move forward in reading. Gifted readers also enjoy the concept of "buying back" time through the use of curriculum compacting and then using that time to work on projects on their reading activity menus.

Read, Rotate, Record

This method of instruction gets the students up and moving—literally! It is often a favorite activity. The teacher chooses a book that the class will read. For example, the teacher chooses two books that relate to art and art appreciation. One book is considered to be on grade level, while the other book is more advanced. Students who are reading on grade level will read the first book, and advanced readers will read the second.

Before students read the books, the teacher places four sheets of large paper around the room. The teacher then shows the book covers and titles to the class. The students *read* the titles and talk about the topic of art and what they think the books may be about. The teacher will then tell the students that they will *rotate* around the room and *record* facts they may know about art. The students keep rotating and adding information to the sheets until the sheets are full of facts and terms related to art. All students will participate; differentiation takes place because students read different books at varying ability levels.

After students read their assigned books, they will then rotate around the room, recording additional information that they learned from their particular books. When the teacher calls the students back into a whole group setting, the group can discuss the information found on the four sheets of paper.

It can also be fun to organize the information on the sheets of paper into further categories. For example, use a yellow highlighter to group information related to art media, and a pink highlighter to indicate information related to artists. Students like seeing the final product. The four sheets of paper for read, rotate, and record might look something like this:

Hatch Strokes Landscapes Color	Pablo Picasso Rembrandt Artists have different styles
Portraits Self-portraits Crayons Markers	Art is fun Art tells a story Art requires skill

Graphic Organizers

A graphic organizer is a way for teachers to get students to process information in a visual format. Students use one of many different graphic layouts to record information about a topic or a book. Graphic organizers help students to "think about thinking." Students who complete graphic organizers begin to compare and contrast ideas and subjects. Using these tools with gifted readers allows them to "chunk their learning" into categories. This helps to promote retention of material as well as expansion of learning.

Merkley and Jefferies (2001) describe five valuable benefits for students when using graphic organizers. These are:

1. verbalizing relationships among visual concepts.
2. providing opportunities for student input.
3. connecting new information to past learning.
4. making references to the upcoming text.
5. seizing opportunities to help students decode and make structural analysis.

Understanding the importance of graphic organizers will encourage teachers to use these new instructional tools in many ways.

How to Use Graphic Organizers

Martha Larkin (1997) offers the following to help teachers implement the use of graphic organizers in their classrooms. Graphic organizers can be used to:

➤ help students locate and remember key facts and ideas.
➤ introduce and/or rearrange text information.
➤ strengthen written and spatial arrangement of information.
➤ summarize text, chapter, and units.
➤ view information as a meaningful whole.
➤ act as study guides.
➤ help see interrelationships among ideas.
➤ provide alternatives for test formats.

Types of Graphic Organizers

For the purpose of this book, I have only included a few examples of graphic organizers. Many more are readily available in other books.

Chain of Events Organizer

This is a graphic organizer that aids in the sequencing process during reading instruction.

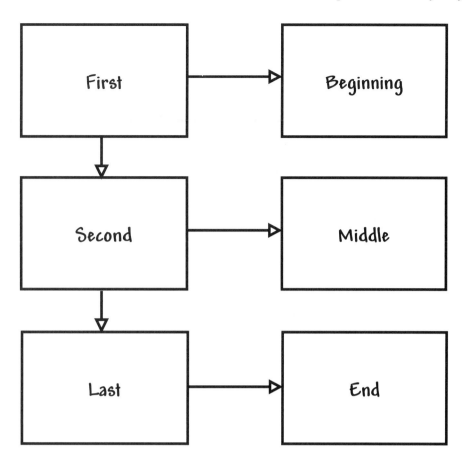

This is an excellent organizer to use with the younger gifted readers. Teachers may choose to have students either write or illustrate their responses.

Storyboards Organizer

This graphic organizer allows students to recall major events and then illustrate them in chronological order, much like a comic strip. This is also a great tool to use with those younger gifted students who seem to be wizards at reading but who lack comprehension skills. Storyboards also help evaluate a character's actions.

Clustering Organizer

This organizer allows students to brainstorm ideas, pictures, feelings, and characteristics about a given vocabulary word, idea, or theme. It may be used as a whole class or an individual activity. It is particularly effective when used to precede writing activities. For example, if the book is about bears, students might brainstorm things we know about bears before reading the book.

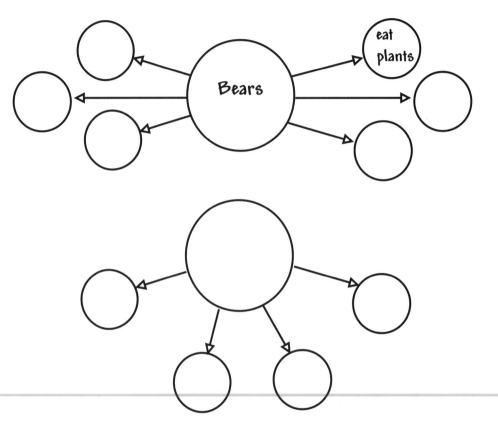

Problem/Solution Organizer

This is an instructional tool that helps to identify problems and consider various solutions.

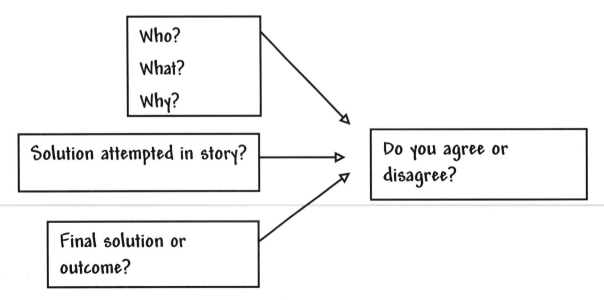

Venn-Diagram Organizer

This popular organizer consists of two or more overlapping circles that allow students to compare and contrast characters, stores, settings, plots, and so on. They may be used as a pre-writing tool to help organize thoughts, or after reading to compare character traits found in the story.

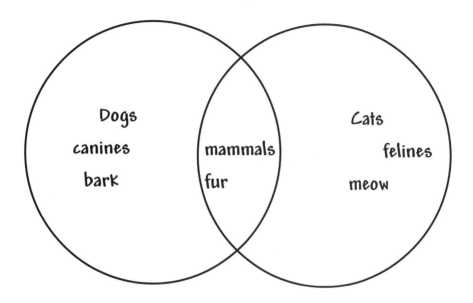

Spider Map Organizer

Spider maps help students graphically portray central ideas and their related aspects.

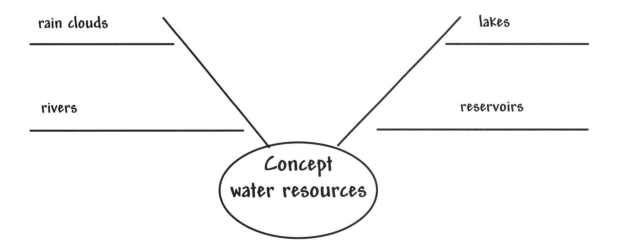

Guidelines for Using Graphic Organizers

Teach gifted readers about using graphic organizers as a way of "chunking" information and organizing their thinking. Explain why these tools are so important. Then:

➤ Provide examples of graphic organizers on chart paper and hang them in the classroom.

➤ Use graphic organizers on a regular basis to encourage student use as well. For example, the teacher reads *If You Give a Mouse a Cookie* by Laura Numeroff. After reading, the teacher can complete a chain of events graphic organizer to help students sequence the events for the story. The teacher can accomplish this by completing the chart on the board while asking the students for their help. After completing the graphic organizer, the teacher then asks the students to write a new story, *If You Give a Dog a Bone*. Students can make graphic organizers prior to writing their stories.

➤ Explain that graphic organizers can be used in small groups, large groups, or individually.

➤ Allow gifted readers time to create and design their own graphic organizers and present their new creations to their peers.

Some educators prefer not to use graphic organizers because they believe that they are similar to worksheet instruction. However, if used properly, graphic organizers give students new ways to see, organize, and extend their thinking. The effectiveness of graphic organizers usually depends upon a teacher's ability to implement them.

Thoughts about Readers and Reading

Butler and Turbill (1987) help us understand what proficient readers do before, during, and after reading a book:

➤ *Before reading a book*: Proficient readers bring to their reading previous knowledge and expectations about the topic, the language used, the sound-symbol system, and the presentation of the text.

➤ *During reading*: Proficient readers typically use skills such as draft reading, skimming, and searching for sense. They use author's cues, predict outcomes, and discuss.

➤ *After reading*: After proficient readers finish a book, they often respond in a variety of ways that include reflecting upon the book. Proficient readers feel success and may want to read the story or book again.

Understanding what gifted readers do before, during, and after reading books helps teachers select appropriate literature pieces and activities that guide gifted readers to analyze, synthesize, and evaluate information. Activities in Chapters 5 and 6 have been developed to promote higher-level thinking and learning. As you read through the next two chapters, you will see how the activities can be adapted to fit into any classroom containing gifted readers. You will also realize that strategies discussed in Chapters 3 and 4 have been in included in Chapters 5 and 6. This will allow you to see how each strategy can be applied and managed.

Let the fun begin!

Key Points

✎ Learning centers provide all readers with skill-appropriate independent activities.

✎ Literature binders are organizational tools designed to allow gifted readers to self-select and monitor their reading activities.

✎ Reading buddies read together, reflect on and respond to their reading, and have fun in the process.

✎ Reading boxes, appropriate for all learners, contain student- or teacher-generated questions about certain books. Student responses go back in the box.

✎ Activity menus, similar to learning contracts, provide a framework for student work and may reflect the multiple intelligences.

✎ Read, rotate, and record allows students to move about as they share knowledge of a topic or their reactions to what they have read.

✎ Graphic organizers can be used in a wide variety of ways and appeal to many gifted readers.

Chapter 5

Books and Activities for Primary Gifted Readers

Putting the right book into a child's hand does not guarantee that the child will engage in it. In order to bring a child and a book together successfully, the child has to make predictions, visualize characters and think with new information.

—Laura Robb

Differentiation Activities for Gifted Readers

Differentiation for gifted readers can be accomplished in many ways (Winebrenner, 2001):

➤ Gifted readers can read books that are based on the same theme as the books read by the rest of the class.
➤ Gifted readers can use study guides and extension activities.
➤ Gifted readers can read self-selected books and complete different learning tasks from their classmates.
➤ For skill work, gifted readers can be given compactors and contracts for a faster pace of learning.

This chapter includes plans and activities relating to a variety of books written for preschool to third-grade readers. The books have been selected in part because they address intellectual as well as social and emotional needs of gifted students. The activities are designed to extend literature for gifted readers and are based on the information and research in Chapters 3 and 4. These activities offer readers further opportunities to respond to literature, analyze information, enhance reading skills, relate information to their own lives, and take responsibility for their own learning.

Further extension occurs when students' social and emotional characteristics are considered. Books may be selected based on themes or characters in them that may be of particular interest to a student. As stated earlier, advanced readers like to read books whose characters are like themselves and who struggle with similar issues or concerns. These books, then, have been selected for their topics or themes, with gifted children—who are often concerned about serious themes—very much in mind. In this way, reading reaches not only the academic needs of the students, but it touches the social and emotional aspects of their lives as well.

Suggestions for Using the Activities

Teachers should carefully review the materials, activities, and projects found in Chapters 5 and 6. They can make a list of stories and their themes so that they can integrate these titles into their own curriculum when appropriate. Teachers can also try one or more of the following to learn more about the gifted readers in their classrooms, including their needs and interests.

➤ Give all students the pre-test that accompanies the basal text series. The students take the test in written form so that you can keep the tests for documentation. Students demonstrating mastery will not have to participate in regular reading instruction. Instead, they will be engaged in a *Literature Links* project.

➤ Flexible grouping is one way to utilize the activities found in this book. Try grouping your advanced readers together. As a small group, the advanced readers will complete selected activities that accompany the story they read. It would be wonderful to hold book discussions with these readers after they all have read the same book.

➤ You may also wish to administer an interest inventory. One good one is *Possibilities for Learning*, in Lannie Kanevsky's *The Tool Kit for Curriculum Differentiation* (1999), which is a survey of learning options to identify what a student likes and dislikes most. Another can be found in the appendix material of Karen Rogers' book, *Re-Forming Gifted Education: How Parents Can Match the Program to the Child* (2002a). Your school district may have additional surveys.

➤ For each title discussed in this chapter and the next, there is a subsection titled "Social and Emotional Needs Addressed." One example of a trait that could appear under that heading might be "Perfectionism." If an advanced reader in your classroom is a perfectionist, you can try to locate books in which a character in the book is also dealing with perfectionism. Reading about how the character deals with this trait can help your student understand how he or she might better deal with his or her own perfectionism. Reading with a goal to assist the child with social and emotional issues is sometimes called "bibliotherapy," or therapy through books. It works best when there is discussion with the child or children (either one-on-one or in a group). Halsted's *Some of My Best Friends Are Books* (2002) explains this recommended process thoroughly and discusses books in which the characters deal with themes or issues common to gifted children, such as perfectionism, being different, feeling alone, making friends, relationships with others, sensitivity, intensity, introversion, concern with moral issues, and more.

Before reading any book, a teacher or parent should "set the stage." You can conduct whole group, small group, or individual discussions before books are read to help determine students' background knowledge. When students are actively involved with a theme before reading a book that deals with that theme, they may be more aware of their own values, beliefs, and understanding of these issues as they read. In the same way, students will gain more from their reading if there is discussion following reading. Gifted readers love to discuss the books they've read with each other or with the teacher as discussion leader. They learn to express their thoughts verbally and to appreciate other points of view from listening to other readers' comments and insights.

Although many of the activities in this book key into the academic side of reading—reading comprehension, vocabulary, and decoding skills—it is important for teachers to know that gifted readers also grow socially and emotionally from reading books in which they identify with the characters or themes. Teachers who implement activities from the current book will no doubt want to refer to Halsted's larger book for additional titles and discussion questions.

Don't Feed the Monster on Tuesdays

by Adolph Moser

Reading Level: Grade 3.0

Interest Level: Grades K-3

Social and Emotional Needs Addressed
- ➤ Drive to understand
- ➤ Identity
- ➤ Perfectionism
- ➤ Relationships with others

Summary: This story should be read with an adult. The simple format makes it easy to follow. The author tells how to replace negative thoughts with positive ones. He discusses perfectionism and the importance of doing your best and not being concerned with winning all of the time. He also helps readers understand the importance of positive self-esteem.

Introduction: Ask the students: "*What is self-esteem? What do you know about self-esteem? List everything you can think of about self-esteem in five minutes.*"

Have students share their responses. Then ask: "*Think about how you feel when you don't win in a game. What is it like? Which is more important: to win or to do your best? Why?*"

Vocabulary

determined

frequently

picky

proud

scold

self-confidence

self-esteem

sly

Implementing the Vocabulary—Pre-Reading Activities: Students will use 3"x5" index cards. On the left side of the card, they will write a vocabulary word. On the right side of the card, they will write the definition for that word. At the bottom they will write a sentence using that word. Students may then place their cards in a box and title it "Vocabulary Bank."

Students can create a glossary of terms found in the story. Write the glossary words in alphabetical order.

Classroom Activity
Skill: Comprehension and Higher-Level Thinking

Questions for Literature Discussion Groups, Journal Entries, Literature Binders, and Tests

1. What does the author mean when he refers to the monster?

2. Do you have positive or negative self-esteem? Why do you think so?

3. Do you ever feel that you have to be perfect? If so, when and why?

4. Predict what could happen in the story if the monster continued to be "fed".

5. Explain the phrase "become a friend to yourself." How might this change a person?

6. Apply what you know to explain why the author talks about an "inner voice".

7. Do you believe you will change in some way after reading this story? If so, explain how you may change.

8. Find some places in the story that are fiction and some that are nonfiction. Why do you think the author used some of each?

9. What do you think is the author's message to his readers? In your opinion, does the author succeed? Why or why not?

10. List five words that you might use to describe the meaning of this book.

11. Evaluate the title, *Don't Feed the Monster on Tuesdays*. Is it a good title? Why or why not? Can you think of any other title that would work for this book?

12. What questions might people have after reading this book?

Classroom Activity

Skill: Evaluating Yourself

Teacher Directions: Have children lie down on a large piece of paper, and have a friend draw an outline of their body. Students will cut out the outline, then write their personal "can-do" and "can't do" statements on the paper. The drawing below provides an example of what students might say that they can or cannot do.

Name:_____Date: _____Teacher:_____

Directions: Use the outline that your classmate drew of you to write statements about yourself. These statements will tell others all about you. We will share these works of art with one another and then display them in our classroom.

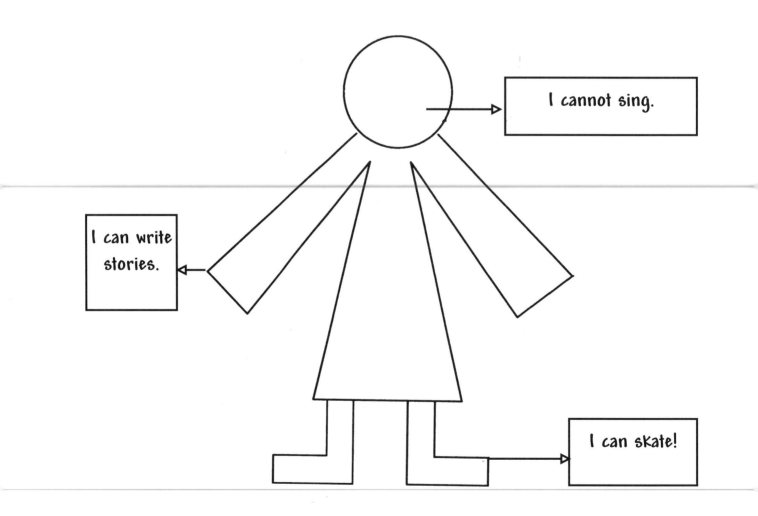

Classroom Activity
Skill: Conducting an Interview

Teacher Directions: Ask your students the following questions and record their responses.

➤ Why is it important that we learn how to interview others?

➤ Where or when have you seen an interview?

I. Definition of "Interview"

An interview is a discussion or conversation between two or more people. Usually one person asks questions (the interviewer) and another person answers them (the interviewee).

II. Purpose for Interviews

1. To gain information

2. To share information

3. To inform people about events, opinions, jobs, TV shows, and performances

III. The Interview Process

➤ Decide on your purpose for conducting the interview.

➤ Select the kind of information you plan to gather. Choose a person to interview who will give you the information you need.

➤ Contact the person you wish to interview; agree on a time and place to meet.

➤ Create a list of questions to ask the interviewee that will help you gather your needed information.

➤ Keep your list of questions brief and to the point.

➤ Arrive on time for your interview.

➤ Make sure all participants are comfortable.

➤ Explain to the interviewee why you are conducting the interview and how you plan to use the information.

➤ After the interview, make sure to thank the person for giving you their time.

Name:_____Date: _____Teacher:_____

Practice Interview: Interview a friend from the classroom. Follow the steps for conducting an interview. Your goal is to find out how your friend thinks about himself or herself.

1. Choose a friend to interview.
2. Decide on a time and place to conduct the interview.
3. Create a list of questions that will help you gather the information that you need.
4. After the interview, complete the graphic organizer that is attached to this page. This will help you organize your information and come to a conclusion about your friend's self-esteem.

Questions You May Want to Ask

➤ Do you believe that you are an interesting person? Why?

➤ What are your special qualities or talents?

➤ Do you have special interests or hobbies?

➤ Why do you like these activities?

➤ What do you consider to be your best accomplishments?

➤ What is your favorite subject in school?

➤ Do you get your homework done on time?

➤ Is there anything about yourself that you don't like or that you would like to change? Why?

Classroom Activity

Skill: Organizing Information

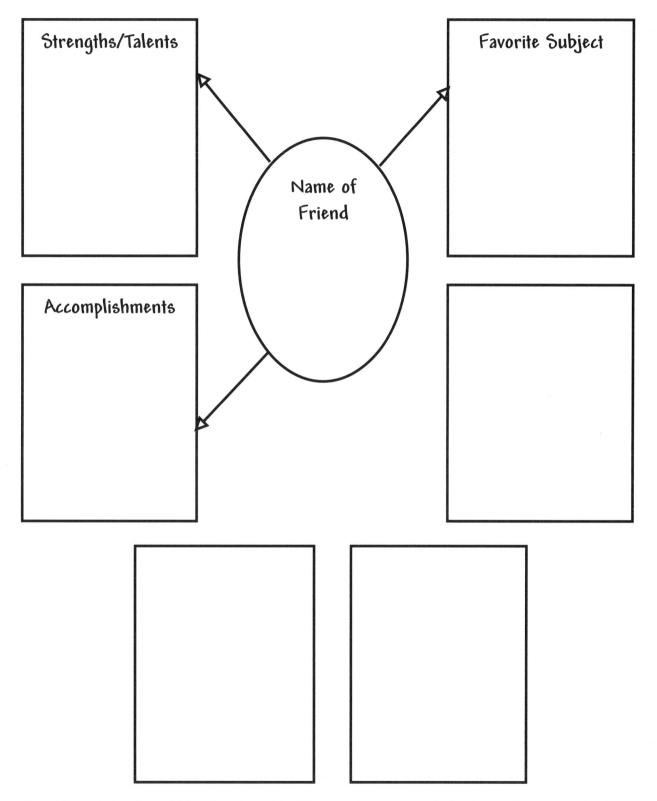

Strengths/Talents

Favorite Subject

Name of Friend

Accomplishments

Abuela

by Arthur Dorros

Reading Level: Grade 3.5

Interest Level: Grades K-3

Social and Emotional Needs Addressed
➤ Developing imagination
➤ Understanding relationships with others
➤ Drive to understand

Summary: This exciting story is about a little girl who is riding on a bus with her grandmother. The little girl imagines that she and her grandmother (Abuela) are carried up into the sky. The story shares what Abuela and the little girl see while flying over the town. The language is rich and includes Spanish words throughout. Each time this story is read, new things can be presented. In-depth discussions can take place using effective questioning.

Introduction: Teachers can introduce a variety of themes through the use of this book. Begin by showing the cover of the book. Ask pre-reading questions: *"What do you think this story will be about? Have you read other stories by Arthur Dorros? What ones? Do you think this story is fiction or nonfiction? What makes you think so? What clues do you see in the pictures that tell us things about the story? Where do you think this story takes place? What makes you think so?"*

Ask students if they have any other predictions about the characters in the story based upon the illustrations. Do they think this story might help us learn about relationships between grandmothers and granddaughters? The story has Spanish words. Do students think this could help teach us about the Hispanic culture? Do students think that this book will be about real things? Make-believe things? Do students know the meaning of the terms "fiction" and "fantasy"? Following the discussion using the questions above, read the book to the whole class.

Vocabulary: The vocabulary in this story can be difficult for students because of the many Spanish words. However, the story does provide English meanings for the Spanish words. Ask students to guess vocabulary word meanings by looking at context clues.

Abuela = Grandma
Buenos dias = Good day
burro
Cerrca del mar = Close to the sea
crane
Cuidada = Be careful
Descansemos un momento = Let's rest a moment
El parquet es lindo = The park is beautiful
flapping
glide
harbor
Hola = Hello

las nubes = the clouds

limonada = lemonade

mangos = mangoes

Me gusta = I like

mira = look

nuestra casa = our house

papayas

patio

Pero quiero volar mas = But I would like to fly more

rodeo

Rosalba = the name of the little girl in the story

Si, quiero volar = Yes, I want to fly

soared

swooping

Tantos pajaros = So many birds

Tia = Aunt

Tio = Uncle

un gato = cat

un oso = bear

una silla = chair

Vamos = Let's go

Vamos a otra aventura = Let's go on an adventure

Vamos al aeropuerto = Let's go to the airport

ven = come

Understanding the Vocabulary: Because the vocabulary in this book is complex, teachers should review words by using context clues and repeated pronunciation. The following are suggestions for teaching vocabulary for this story.

➤ Do not attempt to teach all of the words in one or two days. Take it slow.

➤ Play a game. Make cards that contain one vocabulary word per card. Make another set of cards that contains definitions, one definition per card. Have the students try to match vocabulary words with the correct definitions.

➤ Introduce a few new Spanish words each day. Write them on index cards and place them around the room so that students will become familiar with the words and phrases.

➤ Make small Spanish dictionaries so that students can record their new words and phrases. Even though the words are defined in the story, the students need the added practice and will enjoy having their own personal dictionary to review and keep. Some parents may wish to expand on this idea at home and help the child add more Spanish words to their dictionaries. In any case, the little dictionary will be a memento of a good book read.

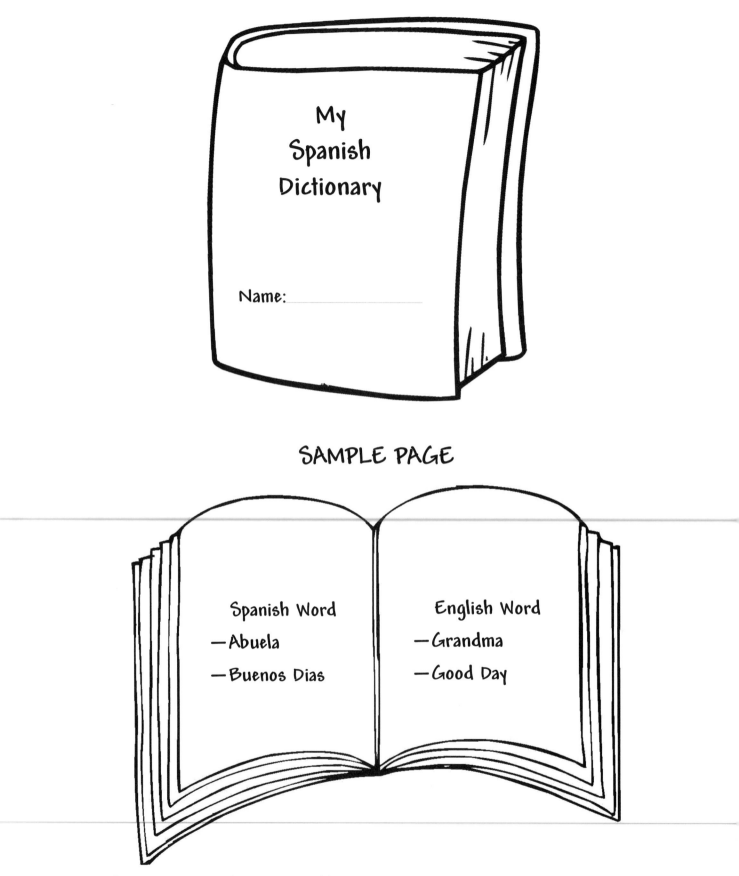

My
Spanish
Dictionary

Name: _____

SAMPLE PAGE

Spanish Word
—Abuela
—Buenos Dias

English Word
—Grandma
—Good Day

Classroom Activity
Skill: Comprehensive and Higher-Level Thinking

Questions for Literature Discussion Groups, Journal Entries, or Tests

1. What does the word "Abuela" mean?

2. What languages do Rosalba and her Grandmother speak?

3. Describe the relationship between the little girl and her grandmother.

4. What do Rosalba and Abuela see in the park?

5. Why does Rosalba think about flying?

6. Why does Abuela like adventures?

7. List some of the places Rosalba and Abuela see while they are flying.

8. What do you feel is the most exciting discovery in the book? Why?

9. Explain what it means to "hook boxes to a crane."

10. Why did Abuela like the Statue of Liberty so much?

11. Do you think that you would like to fly? Why or why not?

12. In what ways does the story teach us about the Spanish culture?

13. What does Rosalba learn while she is with her grandmother?

14. List some ways that speaking a second language could help us in our lives.

Classroom Activity
Using Learning Centers

Teacher Directions: Choose and use the centers that you think will work best with your students. All students need not complete all centers.

1. Abuela and Rosalba spent some time together watching the clouds as they floated by in the sky. Wasn't it fun to learn what items each saw as the clouds passed? Your job is to use blue construction paper and white paint. You will create clouds to form different images. Be creative! Try to think of something original that no one else will think of.

2. This story contains many Spanish words. It is sometimes difficult to learn another language. Play the matching game found in this center to help you learn the Spanish language. There is an answer key in case you get stuck, but I know you can do it!

3. The story of Abuela leaves us with some questions to answer: *Do Abuela and Rosalba ever go on another adventure? Where do they go? Are the two still close after many years? Will they ever fly again, and if so, what will they see?*

4. Imagine that you have the opportunity to write a sequel to this book. A sequel is an extension of the story. It tells us what happened to the characters after the story ended. For example, think about this: Abuela and Rosalba travel to _____ in their new adventure. Tell us where they go and what happens. Can you add some Spanish words to your story?

5. Listening to our own voice on a tape recorder can tell us a lot about how we read. Use the tape recorder in this learning center to record yourself reading the story. Can you pronounce some of the Spanish words? Would you like to send your tape to another classroom so that others may enjoy the story? Remember to use context clues and to vary your reading voice. Have fun!

6. If you like to draw, you will like this center. Using the materials you find in this center, create a picture of your favorite part of the story. After you have completed your picture, cut the picture into medium-size puzzle pieces. Place those pieces into an envelope, and label the envelope with your name. Then leave your puzzle at the center so that others can try to put it back together.

7. Demonstrate that you know the difference between fiction and nonfiction. Make a chart of clues in the story that identify which parts are fiction and which are nonfiction.

8. As Abuela and Rosalba fly high above their town, they see many things. Your job is to imagine that you are flying with these two characters. What do you think you would see? What do you think you would smell? What do your think you would hear? Design a map, a mural, or a chart that would share your ideas with the class.

9. It is always good to send thank-you notes to people after you have spent a nice day with them. Pretend that you are Rosalba, and write a letter to Abuela. In your letter, thank Abuela for the wonderful day. Remember to use proper writing techniques and letter writing skills.

Classroom Activity

Matching Game: English and Spanish for the book *Abuela*

Teacher Directions: Use these cards to play a matching game as a classroom activity or in centers. The blank cards are for adding additional words.

grandma	The park is beautiful.	so many birds	the little girl's name
come	Let's go to the airport.	Be careful.	lemonade
But I would like to fly more.	the clouds	Good day	close to the sea
I like	uncle	aunt	cat
chair	Let's rest a moment.	our house	Hello.
look	Let's go on an adventure	hear	Yes, I want to fly.

Matching Game: Spanish Cards

abuela	El parque es lindo.	tantos pájaros	Rosalba
ven	Vamos al aeropuerto.	Cuidada.	limonada
Pero quiero volar mas.	las nubes	Buenos dias.	cerca del mar
me gusta	tío	tía	un gato
una silla	Descansemos un momento.	nuestra casa	Hola.
mira	Vamos a otra aventura.	un oso	Si, quiero volar.

Frederick
by Leo Lionni

Reading Level: Grade 3.8

Interest Level: Grades K-3

Social and Emotional Needs Addressed
- ➤ Creativity
- ➤ Developing imagination
- ➤ Differentness
- ➤ Identity
- ➤ Introversion
- ➤ Using ability

Summary: Frederick is a field mouse who keeps to himself while the other field mice gather food for the winter. The field mice work all day and night—all except Frederick, that is. When they ask Frederick why he does not work, he says that he works gathering sun rays, colors, and words. Winter comes, and the field mice run out of food. They are hungry and cold, so they turn to Frederick to keep them warm with his sun rays and entertained with his words. This delightful story encourages discussion about acceptance of others who may be different, as well as the value of imagination.

Vocabulary
abandoned
anxiously
applauded
blushed
chatty
daydream
granary
grazed
hideout
reproachfully
shyly

Classroom Activity
Skill: Understanding Vocabulary

Name:_____Date:_____Teacher:_____

Directions: Word chains are graphic organizers that help us think about words and how they are linked to our thoughts and feelings. They also help us associate words with other words. Look at the vocabulary words found in this story. Choose several words to form word chains that show other ideas you may think of because of that word. Example: Use the word *daydream* from the story to create a word chain.

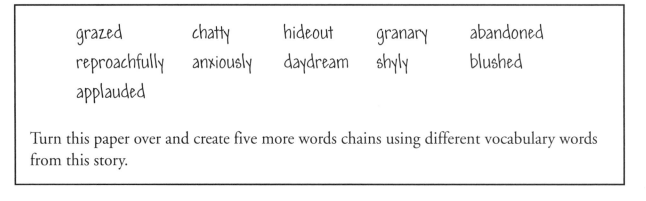

grazed	chatty	hideout	granary	abandoned
reproachfully	anxiously	daydream	shyly	blushed
applauded				

Turn this paper over and create five more words chains using different vocabulary words from this story.

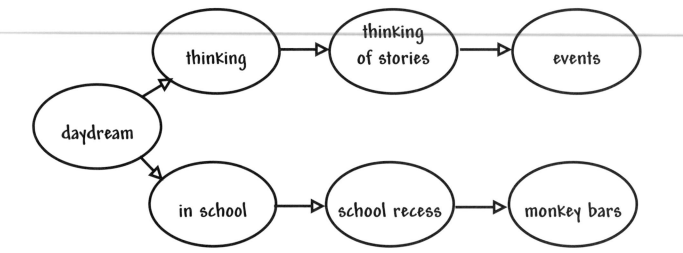

Note to students: This is one way to see how your brain works. One idea helps you think of another. Isn't that amazing?

Classroom Activity
Skill: Comprehension and Higher-Level Thinking

Questions for Literature Discussion Groups, Journal Entries, Literature Binders, and Tests

1. In your opinion, was it okay for Frederick to daydream while the others worked? Why or why not?

2. Frederick was different. He was the only one who thought the way he did. Do you believe that being different is a good thing or a bad thing? Give reasons for your answer.

3. Why did the family of mice begin gathering food?

4. What did Frederick mean when he said that he gathered sunrays for the cold, dark winter days?

5. What did Frederick mean when he said, "I gather colors"?

6. What happened to the food supply as the number of cold, winter days increased?

7. Describe how Frederick was able to help the family through the winter.

8. Why did the family say near the end that Frederick was a poet?

9. What did you like about this story? Are there times when you feel different like Frederick did? If so, explain.

10. How would the story be different if Frederick did not gather his "own supplies"?

Classroom Activity

Skill: Taking Ownership in One's Own Learning

Teacher Note: Susan Winebrenner (2001) suggests using tic-tac-toe menus like this one to help gifted students achieve their goals for choice and independence.

Name:_____Date: _____Teacher:_____

Directions: Pick three activities to complete by _____ (day or date). You must get tic-tac-toe—three in a row—across, down, or diagonally!

Think about groups to which you belong, such as families, clubs, and teams. Describe your role in each of these groups. Complete the worksheet that is attached to this paper.	The illustrations for *Frederick* were done with torn pieces of paper. Using scrap paper found in the classroom, create another illustration that would fit nicely in the story.	Write a letter to Frederick. Give him suggestions for other ways to collect sunrays, colors, and words for the winter. Make suggestions about other things Frederick may want to collect that might help the family during the winter months. Your letter must be written in correct format.
Choose eight words from the vocabulary list. Create a dictionary using the words you selected. Please provide a definition and a sentence for each word.	**FREE CHOICE** Write your own idea in this space.	Leo Lionni has written many other children's stories. Locate another story written by Lionni. Read the story and write a two-paragraph summary. Include your own illustrations. Then tell which story you liked best and why.
What do you know about field mice? Use the computer to locate 10 facts about field mice. Create a poster that you can share with the class that describes what you learned.	How might the story be different if Frederick had not gathered the sunrays, colors, and words? What actions do you feel the field mice would have taken in order to survive? Write a one-page paper explaining your answers.	After reading the story, locate the following: —10 nouns —10 verbs —5 adverbs —2 exclamatory sentences —5 declarative sentences Write your answers and turn them in to the teacher.

Classroom Activity

Skill: Understanding One's Role in Groups

Name:_____Date: _____Teacher: _____

Directions: Frederick and his family had certain responsibilities within their group. Think about your responsibilities in groups to which you belong.

This sheet is to be completed with the activity in the first square of the tic-tac-toe menu. Make a list of groups in which you belong, and then record your roles and responsibilities within those groups. Use the form below to help you.

Groups to which you belong	Your roles	Your responsibilities

Classroom Activity

Tic-Tac-Toe Activity Menu Evaluation

Name:_____Date: _____Teacher: _____

Projects Completed: #_____, #_____, #_____

Skills Being Assessed: _____

_____

_____

_____

| 1 = Poor | 2 = Average | 3 = Good | 4 = Excellent |

Project Numbers _____   Score

Followed directions   1 2 3 4

Completed on time   1 2 3 4

Demonstrated understanding of projects   1 2 3 4

Made connections with other content areas   1 2 3 4

Brought outside information to project   1 2 3 4

Shared projects with class   1 2 3 4

Demonstrated competency in working independently   1 2 3 4

Time of Wonder

by Robert McCloskey

Reading Level: Grade 4.8

Interest Level: Grades K-3

Social and Emotional Needs Addressed
- ➤ Developing imagination
- ➤ Relationships with others: Family members
- ➤ Group discussions help students talk about fears and feelings

Summary: This is a delicate and warm story of a child's summer in Maine. With descriptive language, Robert McCloskey paints an inviting picture of life on Penobscot Bay. The author makes the reader aware of nature, with its gentleness and power. The family weathers a storm together with the help of entertainment and the security of their relationship with each other.

Vocabulary

acrobatic	battening
channel	cormorants
eider	ferns
feuding	gazing
heron	lessening
migrating	mooring
pennants	ripple
rustling	silhouettes
tolling	unfurling
wallows	

Understanding the Vocabulary: Students may use the dictionary to find the meaning of the vocabulary words before reading the story. After they have found the meanings for the words, invite the students to play "Vocabulary Charades." For this game, students pick a word from the vocabulary list to act out for the class. The class then attempts to guess which word the student is acting out. Or you may divide the class into two teams for competitive play.

Classroom Activity
Skill: Comprehensive and Higher-Level Thinking

Questions for Literature Discussion Groups, Journal Entries, Creative and Critical Thinking Cards, and Tests

1. Describe two different times in the story when the author talks about change.

2. List two reasons why you think the author titled his story "Time of Wonder".

3. Explain why the author ended the story with this question, "Where do hummingbirds go in hurricanes?"

4. Have you ever been in a thunderstorm or other kind of large storm? What are some signs that let you know a storm is coming?

5. Name three islands in the story. Why might they have been given their names?

6. When the author used the phrase, "the fog has lifted", what did he mean?

7. Do you think Robert McCloskey has been to Penobscot Bay? Why? Why not?

8. The storm was a hurricane. What damage did the storm do to the island? How might these damages affect the people who lived there?

9. Explain what the family did during the storm. Analyze the family's actions during the storm. Why do you believe they acted in such a manner during the storm?

10. This family reacted to the storm differently than other families might react. Do you believe the storm changed the family's relationships with one another? Explain.

Classroom Activity

Skill: Analyzing Story Passages

Directions: Analyze the following passages found in *Time of Wonder* by Robert McCloskey. Choose three of the five passages and tell what they mean and why they are important to the story.

1. "At the water's edge on a foggy morning in the early spring you feel as though you were standing alone on the edge of nowhere."

2. "On your island you feel the light crisp feeling go out of the air and a heavy stiffness takes its place."

3. "People and papers and Parcheesi games are puffed hair-over-eyes across the floor…"

4. "…the wind whispers a lullaby in the spruce branches…"

5. "It is a time of quiet wonder—for wondering, for instance: Where do hummingbirds go in a hurricane?"

Classroom Activity

Skill: Responding to Literature through Writing

Teacher Directions: Engage students in a whole group discussion using the following prompts:

➤ What are some things in our society that have changed since your grandparents were young? In five minutes, write down as many as you can think of.

➤ How does the understanding of change help people in life?

➤ Think about careers or professions that study change. Why is it important that we understand the concept of change?

Review the elements of writing an essay. Older students should be familiar with this process. Encourage younger students to free-write about changes in their lives. Have they ever moved? In what ways are their lives changing as they grow older?

Use the following activity about change as seat-work or as a learning center project—but only after you have had plenty of discussion and sharing of ideas from the above questions.

Directions: Write a paper that addresses the concept of change. Your essay must contain a topic sentence, supporting details, and a summary.

Use this web to brainstorm ideas for your essay. Make more branches on your web if you need them. After you have completed your essay, attach it to this web and turn it in.

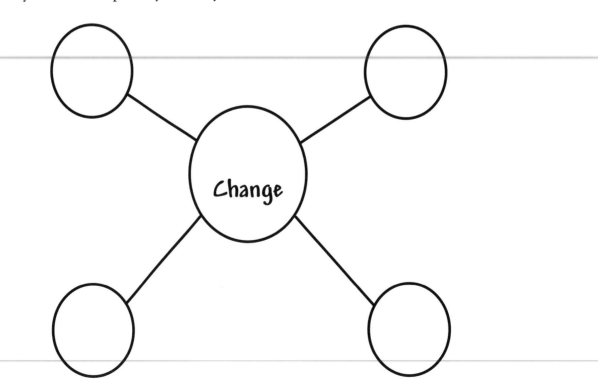

Classroom Activity
Extension Activities

1. Collect objects from your home or from the classroom representing events from the story. Put the objects in a container or a decorated bag. Retell the story using the objects in your container

2. Create a travel brochure enticing others to come to Penobscot Bay. Think about the things that people can do while visiting the island. Make your brochure informative and creative. Remember, you are trying to "sell" the island so that others will come.

3. Pretend that *Time of Wonder* has been made into a television special. Design a print advertisement for the show. Include the name of the book, the author, featured actors, and pictures to encourage others to watch.

4. Write a song that captures the mood of the story. You may want to write the lyrics first and decide on a tune to go with your lyrics. Or you might prefer to come up with a tune, then add the lyrics. You may tape record or perform your song for the class.

Old Turtle

by Douglas Wood

Reading Level: Grade 4.2

Interest Level: Grades K-5

Social and Emotional Needs Addressed
- ➤ Drive to understand: humans' attempts to learn about God
- ➤ Sensitivity
- ➤ Developing imagination

Summary: This wonderful fable for children and adults tells of a time long ago when animals and mountains could speak. An argument occurs as these creatures discuss their different concepts of God. An old turtle stops the argument and convinces the creatures that they are all correct. Old Turtle tells of the coming of people to earth and how they too began to argue about God. In the end, the characters all learn about the beauty of the earth and how everyone has different viewpoints about God and religion.

Note: Judith Halsted recommends this book for gifted readers since one of the characteristics of gifted children is an early interest in religion and spirituality. These are difficult and sensitive subjects to address in the classroom. This story helps teachers reach beyond one specific belief system. It introduces gifted readers to the idea that everyone has different points of view, and if we listen, we can learn from others' views and beliefs. Due to its advanced vocabulary and complex content, this book should be read aloud to younger children. Older children may read this book independently. Questions and concerns may be addressed in discussion.

Vocabulary

advice	antelope	argued
argument	chirped	communication
declared	depths	insisted
lonesome	misused	possess
presence	reflecting	respected
rumbled	separate	soar
thundered	whispered	willow

Understanding the Vocabulary: The following activities will help introduce the vocabulary for this story.
- ➤ Have the students create sentences using as many of the vocabulary words as they can in each sentence. Students will practice reading the sentences in small groups.
- ➤ Invite students to guess the correct meanings of the words using context clues from the story. Then ask them to look up the meanings in dictionaries.
- ➤ Play vocabulary games, matching words with their meanings.

Classroom Activity
Skill: Higher-Level Thinking

Questions for Literature Discussion Groups, Journal Entries, and Tests

1. The author uses Old Turtle to deliver a message. Why do you think that the author chose a turtle to accomplish this task?

2. Discuss the meaning of this passage: "Once, long, long ago…yet somehow not so very long…." What does this mean to you? What questions is this author trying to get you to think about? Explain.

3. The author uses descriptions such as "quiet as the first breeze and gentle as the mountain." How did these phrases help you understand the story?

4. The author tells us that Old Turtle hardly ever said anything. Why do you believe that Old Turtle chose this moment to speak?

5. How do the beautiful watercolor illustrations add to the powerful yet gentle nature of this story?

6. Why do you think Old Turtle said, "Please stop!"?

7. Why might you recommend this book to a friend?

8. Do you believe that "Old Turtle" was wise? Explain.

9, What do you think was the author's purpose for writing this book?

Classroom Activity

Skill: Analyzing Character Traits

Name:	Date:	Teacher:	

Directions: Old Turtle possessed a variety of obvious character traits. He also possessed traits that were not so obvious. Locate places in the story that help the reader understand more about Old Turtle. Write the page number and the words or phrases that provide the information that you have found.

Description of Old Turtle	Things Old Turtle says or does	What do other "Beings" say about Old Turtle?	Make a list of character traits for Old Turtle that you feel are the most important to possess.

Teacher Note: Enlarge this organizer for students who need more space.

Classroom Activity
Skill: Discussion and Thinking Skills

Teacher Directions: Ask the class, "What are some of the groups of things that inhabit our earth?" As the students respond, write their responses on the board or on chart paper.

GROUP: ANIMALS	POSSIBLE RESPONSE: We should learn about animals because they are living things. Animals need food and water. Some animals make good pets; some provide food.
GROUP: PEOPLE	RESPONSE:

Classroom Activity

Skill: Building Vocabulary

Name:_____Date: _____Teacher: _____

Directions: Using the vocabulary from the story, create puzzles as shown below. Cut out the puzzle pieces and mix them in an envelope. Trade the cards with a classmate to complete.

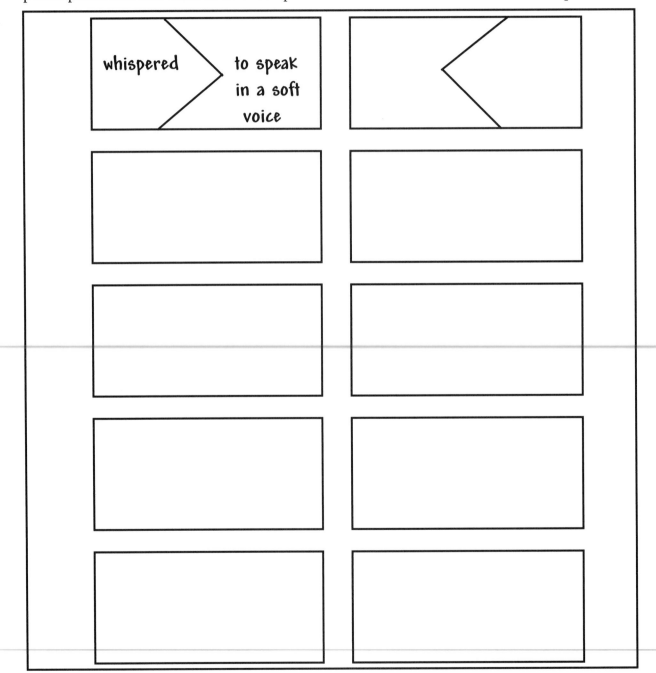

whispered

to speak in a soft voice

Chapter 6

Books and Activities for Upper Elementary Readers

Discussing the story and the illustrations helps a child develop a thoughtful attitude toward reading and facilitates critical, reflective thinking, which is the hallmark of advanced literacy.
—Bertie Kingore

This chapter includes plans and activities relating to a variety of books written for fourth- through sixth-grade readers. As with the books in Chapter 5, these particular books have been selected because they address intellectual as well as social and emotional needs of gifted students, and all are recommended reading in Judith Halsted's *Some of My Best Friends are Books* (2002). Like the activities in Chapter 5, the activities described here offer readers further opportunities to respond to literature, analyze information, enhance reading skills, relate information to their own lives, and take responsibility for their own learning.

Stay Away from Simon
by Carol Carrick

Reading Level: Grade 4.0

Interest Level: Grades 3-6

Social and Emotional Needs Addressed
Drive to understand: "Information helps to reduce fear."
Relationships with others
Feeling different

Summary: An inspiring story about a brother and sister who must examine their feelings about a mentally handicapped boy named Simon. Both Lucy and her younger brother, Josiah, fear Simon but end up feeling differently by the end of the story.

Vocabulary

awkwardly	chinks
cloak	droned
embarrassed	frowned
hastily	murmur
puzzlement	schoolmaster
screeching	sheepishly
shuddered	slate
thicket	

Understanding the Vocabulary: Students may choose from the following activities to practice recognition of the vocabulary found in this story.

➤ Create a word scramble using the vocabulary words. Also develop an answer page. Example: rafe = fear

➤ Create a crossword puzzle using the vocabulary words, and include an answer page.

Classroom Activity
Skill: Comprehension and Higher-Level Thinking

Questions for Literature Discussion Groups, Journal Entries, Literature Binders, and Tests

1. What does this passage mean to you: "His mind goes too slow for schooling"?

2. Why did the children call Simon "Simple Simon"?

3. Parents warned their children to stay way from Simon. Do you believe that this was fair? Explain your answer.

4. If you were Lucy, what would you have done when Simon was throwing snowballs?

5. Why was there a stove in the school?

6. What type of teacher was Master Hume? Why do you think so?

7. Describe Josiah's punishment for not paying attention in class.

8. Did you agree with this punishment? Explain.

9. Where was West Tisbury located? What clues in the story led you to that fact?

10. How did you feel as you read about Lucy and Josiah's walk home?

11. Should Lucy have gone off the path on the way home? Explain.

12. How did Lucy and Josiah feel as they realized that they were lost in the snowstorm?

13. What do you believe Simon was doing as he put Josiah under the large coat?

14. Where did Simon choose to sleep at Lucy's house? Why?

15. How did your feelings for Simon change at this point in the story? Explain why.

16. If you were Lucy, how would you tell the other children about Simon and how he helped you and your brother?

17. What important things did the people in this story learn?

Classroom Activity
Skill: Analyzing Characters

Name:	Date:	Teacher:

Directions: Complete the chart below by locating events in the story that caused reactions from the characters in the story. Then decide why the characters reacted in such ways. An example has been filled in already.

Event	Page #	Reaction from others	Why did these characters act this way?
Simon was watching the other children at the schoolyard.	Found on page 11	The other children tried not to look at him or stare at him.	They were afraid of Simon because of what they had heard about him.

Classroom Activity
Skill: Forming Opinions

Name:	Date:	Teacher:

Directions: *Stay Away from Simon* takes readers through many different events. These situations may be funny, exciting, interesting, or sad. Record your opinions about the story on the chart. Carefully review the story to make your decisions.

Funniest	Why
Most Exciting	Why
Most Interesting	Why
Saddest	Why
Favorite	Why

Classroom Activity
Skill: Research

The 3 R's – A Cooperative Learning Project
Research, Record, Report

Teacher Directions: Divide the students into three groups. The number of children in each group may vary according to how many students read the book. Explain to the students that they will find facts about the 1800s since the story *Stay Away from Simon* was set in the 1800s.

GROUP 1:   Find and record facts about the clothing styles and foods from the 1800s.

GROUP 2:   Find and record facts about the transportation and homes of the 1800s.

GROUP 3:   Find and record facts about the recreation and schools of the 1800s.

After the groups complete the research, they must decide on how to present their findings to the class. They may make a poster, build a model, write a report, make a mobile, or write and illustrate a children's book. Each group member must agree on the project and contribute to the presentation for the class. They must work together to create a presentation that teaches others about the 1800s. *Hint: It helps to discuss roles for each member of the group before they begin working.*

Classroom Activity
Skill: Evaluating Cooperative Learning Projects

Directions: Use the rubric below to help evaluate your research project.

Members in your group: _____

Dates your grouped worked together: _____

Where did you find your facts and information? _____

How did you present your findings? _____

	Excellent	Way to Go!	Acceptable	Needs Improvement
Roles among group members	Roles were assigned at the beginning. All group members performed duties assigned.	All students had roles, but some did not understand their duties.	Some students had roles, while others did not.	Unorganized when assigning roles in group. Group members did not have specific duties.
Interaction among group members	All members interacted by asking questions and offering suggestions.	Most students interacted well. Discussions were helpful.	Only ½ of the group interacted and offered help.	Little to no interaction. Group members worked independently.
Responsibility among group members	All students shared responsibility.	Most students shared responsibility.	Only ½ of the group shared responsibility.	Only 1 or 2 were responsible for completing tasks.
Participation among group members	All students equally participated.	Most of the students participated.	Only ½ of the group members participated.	Only 1 or 2 participated, while the others did not.

Classroom Activity
Skill: Writing

Name:_____Date: _____Teacher:_____

Directions: Many times, people learn from making mistakes. In the story *Stay Away from Simon*, Lucy made mistakes. What do you think Lucy learned, and how do you think her life will be different because of what she learned?

Write a paper that answers these questions. Your paper should include at least three paragraphs. Use the space below to create an outline or a web, and use the back of this paper to write your first draft. Write your final draft on a separate sheet, or use a computer.

Classroom Activity
Skill: Creative Thinking and Production
Extension Activities

Teacher Directions: The following activities can be used in a variety of ways. Refer to Chapters 3 and 4 for more ideas for implementation.

1. Design and create a timeline depicting the events that occur in *Stay Away from Simon*. Can you think of a fun and exciting way to create your timeline?

2. Pretend that you are Lucy from the story. Your job is to introduce Simon to your class. You should write your introduction by telling about Simon's character traits, his hobbies, his background, and anything else that you would like to share.

3. The issue of diversity is found in this story. Locate articles from magazines and newspapers that deal with diversity or people who are different. Create a scrapbook of your articles. Summarize each article that you find in one or two sentences.

4. Use popsicle stick puppets to retell the story of *Stay Away from Simon*. You will need to write the script, as well as make your puppets. If you choose, you may perform your puppet show for the class.

Seedfolks
by Paul Fleischman

Reading Level: Grade 4.3

Interest Level: Grades 4-8

Social and Emotional Needs Addressed
➤ Drive to understand
➤ Moral concerns
➤ Relationships with others

Summary: This book tells of a young girl from Vietnam who, in memory of her father, plants lima bean seeds in a vacant lot. Neighbors notice the beauty of the garden and join her. The author uses the stories of 13 people from different countries and with different dialects to show how to overcome fear and prejudice. *Seedfolks* is an excellent story for gifted readers because the theme offers opportunity for valuable discussions. Advanced readers will enjoy the author's ability to write in different voices, as he speaks through people with different backgrounds.

Vocabulary

altar	alterations	aroma
babbling	billiard	blight
bobbed	bodega	chatted
commanded	coolies	crevices
customary	decisively	declined
decorum	deltoids	dignified
disgrace	dweller	eerie
electrocuted	equation	exploit
foes	furrowed	graduate
Guatemala	haphazard	herring
hoeing	idle	illegally
incense	locket	mending
meteor	notion	nutmeg
obituaries	obliged	pacifism
paradise	pioneers	plantation
pueblo	refuge	Salvadorans
shriveled	solitary	spigot
spit	status	stomped
suspense	suspiciously	swallow
teetered	tio	tremolo
wilt		

Classroom Activity
Skill: Comprehension and Higher-Level Thinking

Questions for Literature Circle Groups, Journal Entries, Literature Binders, and Tests

Teacher Directions: Each chapter in *Seedfolks* is a complete story about one of the neighbors involved in the garden. It is recommended that the following questions be used during literature discussions. You may choose to use only a few questions each day. These questions are suitable for use in mixed-ability classrooms.

1. Kym is a young girl from Vietnam. Describe where she goes each day.

2. Why did Kym have no memory of her father?

3. What does Kym plant in the small holes? Why does she feel that this is so important?

4. Describe the various types of people that live on Gibb Street.

5. Why didn't people stay for very long in the apartment complex?

6. What did Ana see in the vacant lot that surprised her? Why was she surprised?

7. How did you feel when Ana dug up Kym's bean plants? Why did you feel this way?

8. What would you have done if you were Ana?

9. Tell why Ana bought binoculars.

10. Tell what you think this quote means on page 6: "My curiosity was like a fever burning inside me."

11. Why was Wendell so nervous when he heard the phone ring? How do you know?

12. Why did Ana call Wendell in such a panic?

13. Ana was obviously upset about the plants. Why do you believe she felt this way?

14. If you were Kym, how would you have reacted when you saw Wendell tending to the plants? Why?

15. Evaluate why Wendell was willing to help a stranger.

16. How did this event change Wendell's thinking about life?

17. Describe Wendell's actions after he met Kym in the vacant lot.

18. Explain why Gonzalo said, "the older you are, the younger you get when you move to the United States."

19. Describe how Tio Juan acted when he moved to the United States. Why did he act this way?

20. What did Tio Juan discover when he wandered away from the house?

21. Tio Juan was fascinated by the man with a shovel in the vacant lot. What did he do after finding Wendell in the vacant lot?

22. Tio Juan showed Gonzalo how to plant seeds and how far apart the seeds should be. Why did Tio Juan do this?

23. In your own words, tell how the vacant lot changed Tio Juan and Gonzalo's lives.

24. What connections can you make among Kym, Ana, Wendell, Ganzalo, and Tio Juan?

25. Why did Leona's Granny outlive her doctors?

26. Why did Granny lay goldenrod on the graves of her doctors?

27. What led Leona to the vacant lot?

28. The pattern of change is evident throughout the book. Explain how change has affected the lives of the characters this far.

29. Leona describes the vacant lot as a dump. Why do you think City Hall would not clean up the trash? Explain your answer.

30. What actions did Leona take to get the trash removed from the vacant lot? What did Leona learn from this experience?

31. Why did Leona take a bag of trash with her when she met with the city officials? How did it help her prove her point?

32. How did the vacant lot change after Leona's visit to the city officials?

33. Sam considers his job to be "sewing up rips in the neighborhood." This statement has meaning and symbolism. What does this statement mean to you?

34. Why did Sam say, "the garden was a copy of the neighborhood"?

35. Why did the homeless man begin ripping up people's plants in the garden? How did this make you feel?

36. Sam tells about people putting their signs and barbed wire up around their gardens. How will this effect the garden?

37. Why was Virgil's dad amazed by the garden?

38. Explain, "turn the soil."

39. Describe the locket that Virgil found while digging in the soil and how he felt when he found it.

40. Why did Virgil's dad want to plant lettuce?

41. Do you think it was fair for Virgil's dad to use so much of the vacant lot for his garden? Explain your answer.

42. How do you think Virgil felt as his dad kept telling lies to Miss Fleck?

43. Why did Virgil's lettuce die?

44. Do you feel that Virgil had a right to be mad at his dad? Why or why not?

45. Analyze why Virgil spoke to the picture of the little girl in the locket.

46. How did this chapter contribute to the story?

47. Sae Young is the next person to tell about her experiences with the garden. hy does the language in this section differ from the other chapters?

48. Tell about what happened in Sae Young's shop after her husband died.

49. How did this event change Sae Young's confidence about being with other people?

50. Tell about a time when you felt afraid. What did you do?

51. What made Sae Young want to be with people again?

52. Analyze this statement: "Nice people feel good, like next to fire in winter."

53. Tell about some of the ideas that the children submitted to get water to the plants.

54. Develop your own plan for getting water to the plants in the garden.

55. Sae Young feels glad because everyone used her funnels. Why do you believe she felt this way?

56. How did Curtis want to use the garden to "win back" Lateesha's affection?

57. Why did some people call Curtis "field slave" or "share cropper"? How did you feel when they called Curtis these names?

58. Why might have Curtis planted tomatoes for Lateesha?

59. If you were Lateesha, what would you do?

60. Tell three things about Nora that make her different from the rest of the characters.

61. Why did Nora call the gardeners "pioneers"?

62. Nora was the caregiver for Mr. Nyles. Do you care for anyone? Tell about it.

63. In your own words, describe the meaning of "some remembered scent was pulling him. He was a salmon traveling upstream through his past."

64. Why did Mr. Nyles smell the soil in his fingers as he rode home?

65. What did Nora mean when she said that the garden was a "mind altering drug"?

66. Describe the emotions and feelings that the gardeners experienced as they all stood under the overhang during the downpour.

67. "We, like seeds, are now planted in the garden." Can you explain what Nora meant when she said this?

68. Why did Maricela think that people would not like her?

69. Who was Penny, and how did she know Maricela?

70. Explain why Penny got a piece of the vacant lot for the pregnant teens. Do you think this was a good idea? Why or why not?

71. How did you feel as you read about Maricela and her life? If you could give Maricela advice, what would it be?

72. What did Amir think about when he saw the garden for the first time?

73. Analyze this statement: "But the garden's greatest benefit, I feel, was not the relief to the eyes, but to make the eyes see our neighbors." How does this statement add to the theme of the book?

74. Amir tells of several events that allowed the gardeners to help each other. Describe these events.

75. Describe the harvest party that took place in the garden.

76. Amir tells about meeting an Italian woman whom he had met a year earlier. What happened with the two of them when they met again? Why was this meeting different from their first meeting?

77. Florence uses the word "seedfolks." Tell why she used this word and how it was related to her life.

78. Why didn't Florence plant in the garden?

79. Plants grow through nurturing and attention. How are the characters in the story like seeds and plants in a garden?

80. What would your family think of this story?

81. If you could choose only three words to describe this book to a friend, what words would you use?

82. Which character do you believe the garden affected the most in life? Explain your answer.

83. How did the end of the story make you happy, sad, or confused?

84. What parts of the story might relate to your life?

85. Predict what might have happened on Gibb Street if Kym had not planted the bean seeds.

86. Could this story really happen? Give your reasons.

Classroom Activity
Skills: Thinking and Discussion

Teacher Directions: *Seedfolks* lends itself to the implementation of literature discussion groups. See Chapter 3 for more information about literature discussion groups. Flexibility is the best practice when using this instructional strategy. Following are some suggestions for introducing the book, forming and managing literature discussion groups, and extending the theme through appropriately selected activities.

➤ **Introduce the book** to the entire class or to the group who will read it by reviewing vocabulary words. Facilitate a group discussion about the title and how it may lead to an idea of what the story might be about. Explain the dynamics of literature discussion groups, and divide students according to their reading abilities.

➤ **Introduce several books** that have been chosen based on individual needs of the students. Gifted readers are given the book *Seedfolks* to read during specified times. This group of students will be given questions to complete during literature discussion time that require higher-level thinking. Students not ready to read *Seedfolks* and understand its complex story line will be given the opportunity to read a different book. Such flexible grouping allows the teacher to differentiate reading instruction by varying reading content.

➤ **Read the book to the class** over a period of time. After reading the book, divide students by ability to form literature discussion groups.

Classroom Activity
Skill: Debate

Name:_____	Date: _____	Teacher:_____

Mock Trial

Scenario: The city government had decided that the vacant lot on Gibb Street can no longer be used by community members to plant gardens. The city feels that there may be safety issues with the gardens on the property.

Instructions: After listing reasons below, select group members to play the roles in a courtroom. You'll need a judge, two attorneys, and witnesses for both sides. Other students may act as jurors.

Question: Should the government forbid the use of the vacant property for community members? Be ready to give support for your reasons.

Reasons for prohibiting the gardens.	Reasons for keeping the gardens.

Classroom Activity
Skill: Understanding the Story Line

Name:_____Date: _____Teacher:_____

Directions: Judith Halsted (2002) writes, "*Seedfolks* speaks of individuals overcoming fear, prejudice, and emotional shells as they work in their separate garden plots. At first they work alone, but eventually, they begin surmounting language barriers to help each other share their harvest" (p. 338). Can you locate places in the story where fear, prejudice, emotional shells, and language barriers are exhibited? Fill in the chart below.

	Page #	Character(s) Involved	Tell About It
Fear			
Prejudice			
Emotional Shells			
Language Barriers			

Classroom Activity
Skill: Creativity, Writing, and Organization
Extension Activities

Teacher Directions: Activities listed below can be used in a variety of ways. You may assign activities to the students at different points in the story according to their ability levels.

1. **Art:** With a small group or alone, create a mural showing the sequence of changes in the vacant lot as the story continues. Use materials found in the classroom.

2. **Writing:** In your group, identify and discuss the theme of the story. Then create two new chapters that follow after the last chapter of the book. Imagine that each member of your group now lives on Gibb Street and notices the gardens in the vacant lot. How will each of you react? Tell your story in the same manner that the stories were told in the book.

3. **Creativity:** Your literature discussion group will be responsible for creating a travel brochure. This brochure will entice others to come and visit the gardens in the vacant lot on Gibb Street. Your brochure must include:

   ➤ a name for the vacant lot.

   ➤ amount of fee, if any, for people to walk through the gardens.

   ➤ the names of all of the people who have gardens in the vacant lot.

   Be creative. You may include pictures if you wish. Use crayons, markers, and/or the computer to develop a well organized and interesting travel brochure.

4. **Meaning:** Authors usually write a book to tell a story that has special meaning. Why do you think Paul Fleischman wrote *Seedfolks*? Discuss possible reasons in your group. Identify elements in the story that contribute to these reasons, and write them down. Present your findings to the class.

5. **Writing:** Members of your group are newspaper reporters and photographers. Pretend that you live near Gibb Street and have heard of the gardens. Write a newspaper article telling the community about the vacant lot and how it has changed over the months. Present your carefully edited article with illustrations.

6. **Art:** You want others to be interested in reading this book. Design a new cover and cover copy for *Seedfolks*. Include pictures, as well as quotes from the story.

Where Do You Think You're Going, Christopher Columbus?
by Jean Fritz

Reading Level: Grade 5.6

Interest Level: Grades 3-6

Social and Emotional Needs Addressed
- ➤ Drive to understand
- ➤ Using ability to discuss the qualities that Columbus possessed
- ➤ In-depth discussions ask students to analyze traits and behaviors portrayed by Columbus

Summary: This book discusses the voyages of Christopher Columbus and his determination to be the first to explore to the Indies. The author does an excellent job of describing Christopher Columbus' life, including his successes and failures. The historical novel provides students an opportunity to evaluate the struggles experienced throughout history.

Vocabulary

adelanta = forward	calculations
curiosity	expeditions
explorer	Genoa
grudgingly	interpreters
merchants	monstrosities
rampaged	tierra = land

Understanding the Vocabulary
- ➤ Choose a word from the vocabulary list that your teacher has provided. Act out the word for your classmates to guess.
- ➤ What words have you found in this story that you do not understand? Write what you think they mean. Then, using a dictionary or asking the teacher, check to be sure that your understanding is correct.
- ➤ What words or phrases in the story give clues to readers about the time period in which the story takes place?
- ➤ Use index cards to create and play a matching game of vocabulary words and their definitions.

Classroom Activities
Skill: Comprehension and Higher-Level Thinking

Questions for Literature Discussion Groups, Journal Entries, and Tests

1. What did Christopher Columbus think about the way the King of Portugal was trying to get to the Indies?

2. Explain why some of the cargo that Christopher Columbus and his crew took with them might have been important to their voyage.

3. What does "sailed into the unknown" mean?

4. How did perseverance help Christopher Columbus throughout his life? Describe the events that took place because he was so persistent.

5. Why do you believe that Christopher Columbus was confused about the place where they had landed?

6. What happened to the Santa Maria that upset Christopher Columbus?

7. Do you believe that Christopher Columbus was a wise man? Explain your answer.

8. Why did Christopher Columbus change the pronunciation of his name after returning to Spain the first time?

9. Find events or passages in the story that proved Christopher Columbus to be an optimistic person.

10. Why did Christopher Columbus dress in a brown robe, like a monk, to visit the King and the Queen?

11. Why did the people call Christopher Columbus "admiral of the mosquitoes"?

12. Two other explorers appeared in the story. What important roles did they play?

13. What impact did the death of the Queen have on Columbus?

14. Tell about some of the mistakes and miscalculations that Christopher Columbus made as he traveled to different places.

15. Did Christopher Columbus find the New World? Explain.

16. Christopher Columbus set off a "wave of exploration." Explain this statement.

17. Read the following words: ambitious, persistent, and curious. Which do you believe best describes Columbus, and why?

18. Which trip do you believe was the most important for Columbus? Explain your answer.

19. Why do you think Christopher Columbus continued to explore new lands?

20. Do you believe that Christopher Columbus was a successful man? Explain your answer with examples from the story.

21. What in today's world might interest Christopher Columbus?

22. If you were Christopher Columbus, what might you have done differently? Why?

Teachers and students: What additional questions would you include in your response journals?

Classroom Activity
Skill: Responding to Literature Using Journals

Teacher Directions: Provide journals for the students. These could be ready-made or student-created notebooks. Have students tab their journals to divide them into sections by cutting out tabs and pasting them onto the page edges. Then distribute questions to individuals or groups of students. No one student should have to respond to all of the questions. Students can later share their responses in small groups.

Directions: Look at the questions as you read the story. Answer each question by writing your responses in the section of your journal where you believe it fits best. For example, if you answer the question *How did perseverance help Christopher Columbus throughout his life?* you could write about things that took place because Columbus was so persistent in the section of your journal called "My Thoughts and Feelings."

Classroom Activity

Skill: Reviewing Story Elements

Name:_____ Date: _____ Teacher:_____

Directions: Graphic organizers help us organize our thinking into categories. Complete the organizer below by filling in the boxes with information from the story.

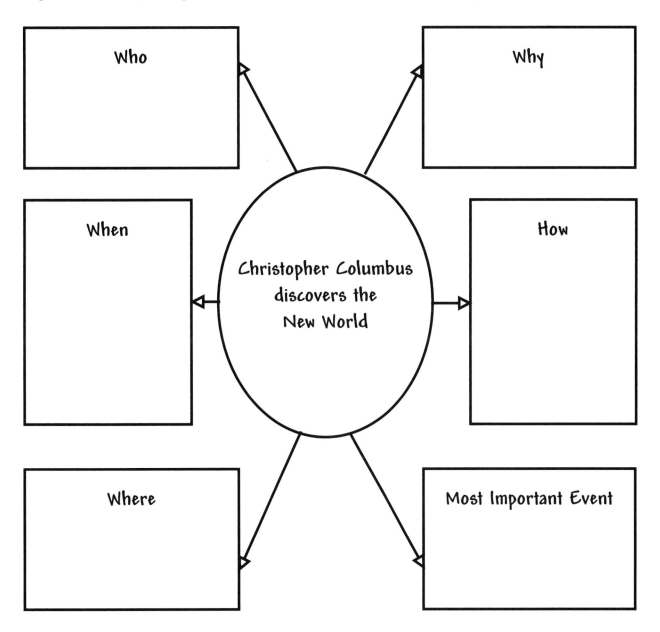

Classroom Activity
Extension Activities

Teacher Directions: These activities may be used for learning contracts, activity menus, or learning centers.

1. **Create a timeline** of the life of Christopher Columbus. Include important information, events, and dates. When your timeline is complete, circle the five events that you believe to be the most significant in Columbus' life. As you share your timeline with the class, tell why you chose those events as the most significant.

2. **Make a visual chart or drawing that describes character traits** that Christopher Columbus possessed. After each trait that you list, record an event or a passage from the book that you feel describes that trait. Below are two examples.

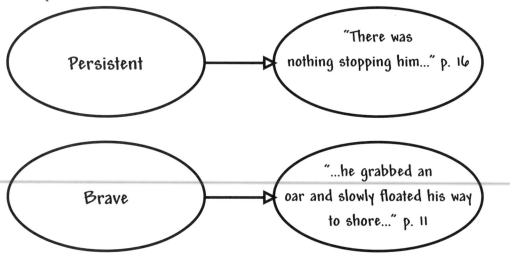

3. **Develop a list of questions** that you would like to ask Christopher Columbus.

4. **Create a coloring book** about this story that would teach younger students about Christopher Columbus.

5. **Construct a map** that would provide details about Christopher Columbus and his journeys.

6. **Create a scrapbook** that would tell others about the life of Christopher Columbus. What items will you include that would help others understand what you have learned? What will you write about Christopher Columbus? Be creative and have fun!

Classroom Activity
Skill: Understanding Fact and Opinion

Name:_____Date: _____Teacher:_____

Statement	Fact	Opinion	Where is it found in the story?

Nothing's Fair in Fifth Grade
by Barthe DeClements

Reading Level: Grades 3-5

Interest Level: Grades 4-6

Social and Emotional Needs Addressed
➤ Differentness
➤ Identity
➤ Relationships with others

Summary: Fifth graders in Mrs. Hanson's classroom learn valuable lessons after an overweight girl joins their class. The author creates believable characters who experience real-life problems. This book can help gifted readers understand differences among their classmates. It may also promote discussions with gifted readers about their relationships with others.

Introduction: The teacher should create an atmosphere of curiosity by asking questions like these: *"Can you think of a time when you felt different from other students at school? How would you feel if someone teased you about the way you look? What might you do if you had a friend that was having trouble at home? What does 'sometimes life is unfair' mean? Discuss the title of the book and how it might relate to the story."*

Encourage the students to think about this concept: *Sometimes we perceive others as being mean or nasty. We need to ask ourselves, "Why are they acting that way? How might we help?"*

The activities for *Nothing's Fair in Fifth Grade* are designed to be incorporated into literature binders (see Chapter 4). Students will work independently or in small groups.

Elements to Be Kept in Literature Binders
Section 1: Overview, Timeline, Goals

Name:_____Date: _____Teacher:_____

Dear Students,

We will be reading *Nothing's Fair in Fifth Grade* by Barthe DeClements. You will be excited to know that we will all work independently as well as in small groups. Your literature binder will help you as you read from the book and complete activities that will help you think about ideas in the book.

We will complete this novel unit on _____ (date). If you have questions during this time, I will be available to help you succeed.

It is important for you to set goals as we explore this piece of literature. Please use the space below to help you think about your goals as you read. Please list three goals.

1._____

_____

2._____

_____

3._____

_____

Elements to Be Kept in Literature Binders
Section 2: Vocabulary Activities

Directions: The following terms are found in the story. Feel free to add or delete words as you feel necessary.

billowed	hovered	blubber
gross	squished	bombarded
wadded	scrounge	antics
thaw	sift	pursed
pranced	herded	trooped
sarcastically	crossly	lugged
davenport	coax	strict
fumbled	lavatory	heaved
intently	tutor	quaky
tangible	bawl	bustling
parole	scoffed	pawed
clamored	reluctantly	halt
snickered	rapped	errand
shivered	tavern	sternly
lolled	persisted	anxious
shooing	wistfully	fiddling
mussed	exemplary	

Other words:

Vocabulary Activities

1. The author uses strong terms such as "fat" and "gross" to describe Elsie at the beginning of the story. How does this language add to the storyline?

2. List words as you read that you consider to be "touchable." This means words that make you see the story better. Choose words that are descriptive and strong.

3. Did you have an image of Elsie throughout the book? How does the author use language (words) to create images? Describe your image of Elsie because of the words used by the author.

4. Using a sheet of paper, make a chart with columns that will help you keep track of the terms found in the story.

   ➤ Words that confused me
   ➤ Words that made me laugh
   ➤ Words that made me sad
   ➤ Words that would hurt others
   ➤ Words or sentences that would help heal feelings
   ➤ Powerful words
   ➤ Descriptive words

5. Choose 15 words from the vocabulary list. Locate definitions for these words. Create a memory game using paper. Cut out small squares and write a word on one square and a definition on another square. Follow this format with the 15 words that you chose. Mix the squares up and then try matching the definitions with the words. Place your cards in an envelope so that others in the class may play your memory game.

6. Create a dictionary using 15 words from the vocabulary list. Be creative as you make your dictionary.

7. Pick several friends who have read the book. Play vocabulary charades by acting out the definitions of some of the words from the vocabulary list.

8. Create a crossword puzzle using several of the words located on the vocabulary list.

9. Create a "true and false" game that you can use with your classmates. Ask them: "The word _____ means _____. True or False?"

10. Pick 10 words from the vocabulary list. Make a word search, and then give it to a friend to complete. Make sure you have an answer sheet.

Elements to Be Kept in Literature Binders
Section 3: Literature Discussion Questions

Teacher Directions: The questions listed below can be photocopied and included in a literature binder. Assign given questions during specific chapters of the book. Pick and choose the questions that best meet the needs of your students.

The Fat Blond Girl

1. Why did the children in Mrs. Hanson's class act the way they did when Elsie walked into their classroom?

2. This chapter is full of words that describe Elsie. How did you feel as you read these unkind words? Why did you feel this way?

3. Why did Mrs. Hanson ask Jennifer to help Elsie around the school?

4. Elsie asked Jennifer and Sharon for food from their lunch trays. Why did the author include this in the story? Why is it important to the storyline?

5. Elsie does not participate in gym. Why do you believe that Elsie chose not to participate?

A Sports Car Only Holds Two

6. Elsie keeps her head down and won't look at adults. Why do you feel she does this?

7. How did you feel when Mrs. Hanson made Elsie spit the cake out in front of the whole class? If you were Mrs. Hanson, how would you have handled the situation?

8. Describe how Marianne treated Elsie.

9. Imagine and describe how Elsie must have felt when her mother said that her car only holds two people.

10. What type of relationship existed between Elsie and her mom?

The Finger Points

11. Explain what happened to everyone's lunch money in Mrs. Hanson's classroom.

12. Do you believe that someone was taking the money? Why do you feel this way?

13. Have you ever lost money? Did you find it again?

14. Analyze Mrs. Hanson's actions as she looked through Richard's desk and Jennifer's purse. Do you feel that these actions were fair to those students? Explain your reasoning.

To Catch a Thief

15. Why was Diane so upset when she saw Elsie coming out of the school when everyone else was outside for recess?

16. Tell about Jennifer's relationship with her mom.

17. How did Mrs. Hanson speak to the class after Lester's money disappeared?

18. Who did Jennifer see at the 7-11? What was this person doing when Jennifer saw her at the store?

19. Jennifer's father said, "…all circumstantial evidence," when he talked about the money being stolen. What did Jennifer's father mean?

The Office Jail

20. If you were Jennifer, would you have told Mrs. Hanson about Elsie buying candy at the 7-11? Tell why you feel the way you do.

21. List three words to describe the conversation between Elsie, Diane, Jack, and Lester when they accused Elsie of stealing their money.

22. Why is this chapter called "The Office Jail?"

23. Why was Jennifer jealous of Elsie when she got 100s on her papers in school?

24. We learn more about Elsie and her old school in this chapter. What other problems did Elsie face at her old school?

The Girls Can't Dance

25. How do you think Elsie felt when no one picked her to dance during gym class? Has anything like that ever happened to you? How did you feel?

26. Jack and Lester laughed at Elsie when she danced. If you were Elsie, how would you have handled the situation?

27. Why did Mrs. Hanson call the students to her desk before giving out report cards?

28. Elsie seemed to talk more with Jenny in the bathroom. Why do you feel she chose to talk to Jenny more at that time?

29. Many unfair things happened to Elsie during her life. Discuss some of the unfortunate things that happened to her. Evaluate why these things happened to her.

30. This chapter seems to contain a turning point in the story. Can you identify this turning point?

31. The author tells us that Elsie often "yanks" on her hair. Analyze why Elsie might pull her hair when faced with different situations.

32. Jenny tells her mom that she would like to hire Elsie as her math tutor. How will this change their relationship?

Money's Gone Again

33. Jenny's mother said that Elsie was the "fattest" girl she had ever seen. Do you feel that this was proper for an adult to say about a child? How would you feel if your mother said that about one of your friends?

34. Why did everyone blame Elsie when they heard that money was missing again?

35. Elsie felt sad after Mrs. Hanson searched her for the missing money. Why did Elsie feel so sad?

36. Elsie did not help Jenny with her math the night before the test. Why do you think Elsie did not help?

37. Tell about the announcement that Mrs. Hanson had for the students about the missing money.

38. Jenny's mother was very excited about her grade on the math test. She offered to take the girls for ice cream. Elsie said she could not go because she was on diet. Did this surprise you? This tells us a lot about Elsie and some changes in her life. What did you learn about Elsie?

39. If you could change places with Elsie or Jenny, which would you choose and why?

40. Jenny made this statement, "The more I know Elsie, the more I forget she was fat." Evaluate this statement and how it is important to the theme of this story.

41. Jenny visited Elsie at her home. Explain what Jenny learned about Elsie's mother during this visit.

The Slumber Party

42. Describe the slumber party at Diane's house.

43. In your opinion, why did Elsie's mother say that Elsie could come to the slumber party after dinner and leave before breakfast?

44. The girls ask Elsie how she got so fat. Would you ever ask someone that question? Why or why not?

45. Diane's mother wanted to make Elsie new clothes. Why do you feel that this was important to Diane's mother?

46. Tell what Elsie gave to the girls at the slumber party.

47. Why do you believe that it was important for Elsie to give the girls gifts at the slumber party?

48. How did Sharon react to Elsie's gift?

49. Tell about Elsie and her feelings about going to boarding school.

50. How did Elsie's mother react to Elsie pants being altered by Diane's mother? Why did the author choose to include this event in the book?

51. If you were Diane's mother, how would you have reacted to the phone call from Elsie's mother? Do you think Elsie's mother had the right to call Diane's mother?

Daddys Don't Wear Aprons

52. Elsie learned a great deal from her new friends. Analyze what Jenny, Diane, and Sharon learned about life from Elsie.

53. Tell why Jenny's father was so upset about her mother working on Fridays and Saturdays.

54. Do you think it was fair for Jenny's father to not help around the house? Explain your answer.

The Hitchhikers

55. The girls decided to walk to the mall. Do you think that this was a wise decision? Why?

56. Diane put her thumb up when the truck passed. Why did she do this?

57. Why do you feel that Elsie was nervous about getting in the back of the truck?

58. If you were walking with the girls, would you have gotten in the truck? How would you have handled the situation differently?

59. Imagine why the girls felt so scared as they rode in the back of the truck.

The Outcast

60. What happened to Elsie's sister when everyone else jumped out of the truck? How did Elsie feel?

61. After Diane's mother arrived at the police station, Diane told her almost the whole story. What part of the story did Diane leave out? Why?

62. Describe how Elsie's mother reacted when she arrived at the police station. How was it different from the other mother's behavior?

63. This chapter teaches the girls a valuable lesson. What lesson did the girls learn?

64. Peer pressure can often bring trouble between friends. Tell how peer pressure played a role in this chapter.

Cats Go Out at Night

65. If you were Jenny's parents, what would you have said to her after leaving the police station? Why?

66. Why do you think Jenny's parents began arguing about bowling and her mother's job?

Peace Talks

67. What did the truck driver tell the police about his purpose for taking the children on the long ride? Did you believe his story? Why?

68. Explain whether you think it was fair for Elsie's mother to give up on her.

The Old Lady Winked

69. Elsie was not only changing by losing weight, she was changing in other ways. Tell about these changes.

70. Why did Elsie begin pulling her hair again?

71. Why do you believe that Mrs. Hanson winked at Jenny when they entered the classroom?

72. How will Elsie get to stay at the school instead of going to a boarding school?

I Can See My Shoes

73. How did Jack react to Elsie as she tried to play softball? What would you tell Jack if you were there?

74. Describe what Elsie did to Jack when he was teasing her?

75. Jenny begged Jack to tell the teacher that it was an accident when Elsie hit him with the bat. Why do you think she did this?

76. If you were Mrs. Hanson, how would you handle this situation, knowing that Elsie would have to go to boarding school?

77. Jenny's mother also made changes in the story. How did Jenny's mother change?

78. Did Jack tell on Elsie? Why do you think he made this decision?

79. The last page of the story tells about the girls' new relationship. How does this page relate to the author's purpose for writing the book?

80. How might this book help others?

81. What surprised you the most in this story?

82. What techniques did the author use to help make the story more powerful?

83. Identify a character that you feel is most like you. Tell why.

Elements to Be Kept in Literature Binders
Section 4: Extension Activities

Teacher Directions: The following activities may be reproduced and placed in literature binders. You may choose to use the activities in various ways. For instance:

➤ Assign numbers to the activities. Then mark the activities that you would like students to complete based on their individual abilities.

➤ Allow students to choose two activities from the list to complete in a given amount of time.

The important thing to remember is not to assign all of the activities listed below. This would be overwhelming.

1. Many people keep diaries to help them remember things that happen to them throughout their lives. Elsie certainly had many things happen to her during her days at different schools. **Create a diary** as if you were Elsie. Your diary should include entries that tell about Elsie at the beginning of the book, the middle, and the end.

2. **Develop a new character** for this story. This character will change the ending of the story. Use details and descriptive words. Include such information as the new character's name, actions, and emotions. Your story extension should include at least three paragraphs. You may choose to write out this assignment or use a computer.

3. **Write a letter to Elsie** encouraging her to continue losing weight. Give her advice on how to deal with her mother. Tell her about trouble you may be having in school, and ask for her advice

4. Cover a cereal box with construction paper. On each side, you will **summarize the events in the story**, as well as story elements. One side will include a list of characters found in the story, one side will include a description of the settings found in the story, one side will summarize the theme that is found in the story, and one side will show how the story changed your own thinking about issues in your life and your relationships with some of your friends.

5. **Create character sketches** of Jenny and of Elsie. Using drawing paper, draw a portrait of each of these characters. Then, write words around each of your drawings that describe their personalities and actions.

6. **Create a timeline** that shows the sequence of events in the story. Be sure to include important events from the beginning, middle, and end of the story. Include the part of the story that you consider to be the turning point, and highlight this part by circling it on your timeline. You may draw pictures on your timeline that will help others better understand the story. When you are finished, choose one event that you think is the most important to the story and tell why you feel this way.

Freaky Friday
by Mary Rodgers

Reading Level: Grade 5.1

Interest Level: Grades 5-8

Social and Emotional Needs Addressed
- ➤ Achievement
- ➤ Using ability
- ➤ Identity
- ➤ Relationships with others

Summary: This is a wacky story about a girl named Annabel who has a fight with her mother, then wakes up the next morning and realizes that she and her mother have somehow traded places. Annabel is now her mother, and her mother is Annabel! The author explores the generation gap as a teenager "walks in her mother's shoes" for a day.

Vocabulary

ambivalent	amiable
annoyed	commensurate
concede	coyly
deplorable	diligent
forlorn	ghastly
imagining	indignantly
loathe	lemmings
nuisance	phosphates

Understanding the Vocabulary

- ➤ Enter these words and others from the story into a vocabulary journal or personal dictionary.

- ➤ Divide the class into small groups. Each group will be responsible for a different vocabulary activity. For example, one group will look the words up in dictionaries while the other groups are creating sentences or drawing illustrations to match the words. All groups meet as a whole to share their findings.

Classroom Activity
Skill: Comprehension and Higher-Level Thinking

Questions for Literature Discussion Groups, Journal Entries, and Tests

Chapter 1

    1. How old was Annabel when she changed places with her mother?

    2. What does Annabel call her young brother?

    3. Describe the relationship between Annabel and her mother in this chapter.

    4. Is this story based on fact? How do you know?

Chapter 2

    5. Describe how Annabel woke her father.

    6. Do you believe that Annabel should have told her father her true identity?

    7. Do you believe that her father should have been suspicious? What parts of the story led you to this understanding?

Chapter 3

    8. How was it confusing for Annabel to get breakfast for everyone?

    9. When did Annabel realize that her mother had changed lives with her?

   10. Describe how Annabel's mother was acting as she was "Annabel" getting ready for school.

   11. How did Annabel feel about kissing her brother goodbye? Why?

Chapter 4

   12. How did Annabel feel about the peace and quiet she got after the kids left for school?

   13. Describe the conversation Annabel had with her father about money.

   14. What is Annabel learning about her mother that she did not know before? Explain your answer.

   15. How would you have handled the conversation with her father?

   16. Why did Annabel want to go to dinner and the movies with her father?

Chapter 5

   17. Why was Annabel embarrassed as Boris looked into her room? Why do you think she acted this way?

   18. Why was Annabel trying to convince Boris to come back and see her when she returned to normal?

   19. Evaluate what Annabel learned about herself while talking with Boris. Why do you believe this?

   20. What happened to the washing machine?

21. Why do you believe that the author chose not to tell readers about "Mother's Day as Annabel" at this point in the story?

22. Who called Annabel when the washing machine went crazy?

23. Evaluate why Annabel told her grandmother that the family would visit her for the entire month of July.

24. Explain the words, "I do not pick up pigpens."

25. Explain this passage: "A kid that's got no discipline is the fault of the mother and father." Do you agree? Explain.

26. Why did Annabel fire Mrs. Schmauss?

27. How can false accusations hurt someone?

28. What happened to Annabel's little brother that made him so upset?

29. Annabel learned something very important about her little brother in this chapter. Describe this revelation.

30. At this point, before reading any further, make a prediction in your journal. Do you believe the conversation that Annabel had with her little brother will have an impact on their relationship later in life?

Chapter 5

31. Explain "I do not pick up pigpens."

32. Explain this passage: "A kid that's got no discipline is the fault of the mother and father." Do you agree? Explain.

33. Why did Annabel fire Mrs. Schmauss?

34. How can false accusations hurt someone?

Chapter 6

35. What happened to Annabel's little brother that made him so upset?

36. Annabel learned something very important about her little brother in this chapter. Describe this revelation.

37. At this point, before reading any further, make a prediction in your journal. Do you believe the conversation Annabel had with her little brother will have an impact on their relationship later in life?

Chapters 8 and 9

38. Describe what Annabel must have been thinking as her father called and told her that he had invited company for dinner.

39. Who did Annabel get to babysit for her littler brother while she went to the meeting at school?

40. If you were Annabel, what would you have done differently during the conference with the teachers?

41. What do you believe that Annabel learned about herself during the conference? Why do you think so?

Chapter 10

42. Why did Annabel call the police?

43. Who do you believe "kidnapped" Ben? Why do you feel this way?

44. Why do you believe that Annabel told the police that she was in her mother's body? Why at this point? She had kept it inside for so long.

45. In your reflection journal, predict what relationship Annabel and her mother will have later in life.

46. Tell about a time when you wished you were someone else. Why did you feel this way?

47. Explain how Annabel's mother returned to the family.

48. What lessons did Annabel learn from her experience as her mother.

Chapter 11

49. Describe how Annabel's mother spent the day as Annabel.

50. What did Annabel write about in her overdue paper?

51. Why is the title of this story *Freaky Friday*?

52. Predict what you could learn if you changed places with your mother or your father.

53. If you could change places with someone else, who would it be and why? What do you think you would learn from the experience?

54. Think of other funny events or situations that could have happened in the story.

55. Do you consider Annabel to be a dynamic or static character? Defend your position.

Note: A character that changes and grows because of an event or events in a story is considered to be dynamic. A character that basically stays the same throughout the story is considered to be static.

Classroom Activity
Skill: Comprehension and Comic Strips

Name:_____Date: _____Teacher:_____

Directions: Comedy is found throughout the story *Freaky Friday*. Your assignment is to create several comic strips that illustrate the funny events that take place in the story. Use the patterns below to help you with your comic strips. If you choose, you may share your comics with the class. Add text and colorful illustrations.

Classroom Activity
Skill: Extending Literature
Extension Activity Menu

Name:_____Date: _____Teacher:_____

Directions: Choose two activities from the menu to complete by _____ (date).

1. Tricky Tuesday, Wacky Wednesday, Silly Saturday…. Choose one of the days of the week and create a story that tells about your very own mixed up day. You change places with someone else. You can travel through experiences that teach you many of life's lessons. Your story should be at least _____ pages and should include illustrations. We will read these as a class and determine what lessons were learned in your story.

2. *Freaky Friday* contains many difficult words. Choose 10 words from the vocabulary list or from the story. Use the thesaurus to find words with the same meanings that could replace the words in the story. These words must not change the meaning of the sentence. Write the sentences with the new words in your journal or personal dictionary. Try to do five words with sentences.

3. In a group of three, create a TV talk show in which group members interview Annabel and her mother. Make at list of questions, and decide who will play Annabel, the mother, and the person doing the interview.

4. When Annabel traded places with her mother, she learned how others saw her. Create a list of events in the story that help Annabel learn more about herself. After creating the list, pick one that you feel is the most important thing Annabel learned and how it will help her later in life.

5. Make a list of several different things that you do that annoy your parents and your siblings.

6. Have you seen the movie *Freaky Friday*? Tell how the book and the movie are alike and how they are different. You may choose to write a paper about this or give a short talk to the class.

7. Pretend you are a salesman for this book. Write a speech that you could give at a "back-to-school" night at your school. Your speech should entice others to buy this book.

8. What questions do you think people might have after reading this book 25 years from now? Write your questions on a sheet of paper.

Classroom Activity
Skill: Understanding Story Elements

Name:_____Date: _____Teacher:_____

Directions: Complete the graphic organizer below by using information from the story.

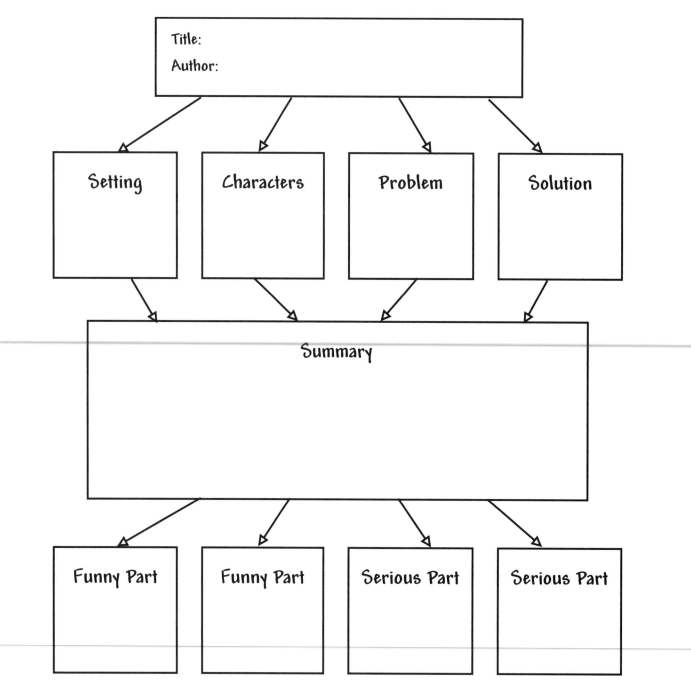

Chapter 7

Assessing the Gifted Reader

While teachers employ many useful strategies to chart student tasks and growth, it is important to recall that the two-fold purpose of all assessments is (1) to chart student growth in regard to valued skills and knowledge and (2) to use information gathered through that process to plan the most appropriate learning experiences possible for given individuals and groups of students.

—Carol Tomlinson

Most students—including gifted students—want to know how they will be evaluated. How many times have we heard, "Will this be graded?" or "Will we have a test on this?" When a classroom teacher uses trade books with gifted readers, the teacher must find or create assessment tools and strategies that will accurately measure student progress. A variety of assessment procedures are possible. All are effective for gifted readers and can be adopted when trade books replace basal readers in the classroom. This chapter provides some examples.

Assessment Strategies Come in Three Forms

Assessment strategies come in three main forms.

Teachers Evaluate Students

Teachers observe student progress in order to document strengths and weaknesses and to plan for effective teaching and learning.

Students Evaluate Themselves

Students learn to make critical decisions as they reflect on their own learning and progress. Self-assessment motivates students to take ownership in their life-long learning.

Students Evaluate Each Other

When students evaluate each other, they learn to offer positive feedback based upon given criteria. When students evaluate other students, everyone who is involved benefits.

Each of these forms has distinct uses and advantages. Alternative assessment strategies—such as portfolios, checklists, and rubrics—are often more effective than traditional testing, because such assessment serves as a diagnostic tool that helps to promote teachers' instruction. Alternative assessment allows students to demonstrate their understanding of given subjects in greater detail. Students who are given opportunities to choose alternative assessments begin to use higher-level thinking skills, including the ability to reflect, analyze, and make judgments

Traditional testing often offers quick "snapshots" of student progress. Feedback from alternative assessment may be more valid, because the information has been gathered over longer periods of time and has taken student learning styles into consideration. The assessment strategies in this chapter are designed to help teachers monitor student growth, achievement, and attitudes.

Many of these strategies can also be used to pre-assess student abilities. Pre-assessment is vital for addressing the needs of advanced readers (Kingore, 2002a). Pre-assessment:

➤ determines students' instructional reading levels and skills.

➤ sorts students according to readiness and the skills that need to be learned.

➤ analyzes students' application of reading strategies.

➤ provides information for selecting appropriate instruction materials and the pacing of those materials to meet students' needs.

The following assessment strategies are flexible and versatile.

When Teachers Evaluate Students

Checklists

Checklists help teachers to "check things off" in the course of observing a behavior, skill, or performance. Checklists can be used:

➤ along with other types of assessments.

➤ as random checks throughout the school year.

➤ to determine appropriate grouping strategies for projects and activities.

➤ to provide reliable information without taking too much time.

Checklists are appropriate for all subjects and with all students. Here are some helpful checklist guidelines:

➤ Create questions and statements that can be answered easily and quickly.

➤ Use short phrases, symbols, or the words *yes* and *no*. If you have to write a lot, your observations may not be as accurate.

➤ Designate an area on each checklist for brief comments.

➤ Make sure your students fully understand how you will use the information gathered from the checklist. Will the information gathered count toward a grade?

➤ Keep your checklists in convenient areas with a clipboard, folder, and pen or pencil.

Some cautions when using checklists:

➤ Do not overuse checklists in your classrooms.

➤ Do not base grades on a single checklist. Checklists should be used to support grades, not to determine them.

➤ Do not use checklists for all subjects at one time. Incorporate the use of checklists slowly, allowing students to become comfortable with this alternative assessment tool.

➤ Do not make checklists too long; the information will not be as valid.

Following are some simple checklists designed to give you ideas for creating your own.

Checklist to Assess Work Habits

Yes ✔ No	Student:	Teacher Notes
	Sets goals	
	Completes tasks	
	Works independently	
	Is prepared for conferences	

Checklist to Assess Summarizing Information

Yes ✔ No	Student:	Teacher Notes
	Summarizes the main idea	
	Uses key vocabulary	
	Has a sense of order	
	Includes the author's purpose	

Checklist to Assess Journal Entries

Yes ✔ No	Student Entries:	Teacher Notes
	Are thoughtfully written	
	Demonstrate appropriate grammar	
	Pose questions	
	Provide answers to questions	
	Follow directions	
	Are elaborated	

Checklist to Assess Attitudes toward Reading

Yes ✔ No	Student:	Teacher Notes
	Is enthusiastic about reading	
	Enjoys reading independently	
	Expresses a desire to read aloud to the class	
	Spends free time reading	
	Encourages others to read in class	
	Expresses concern when not given time to read in class	

Rubrics

Rubrics measure performance using specific criteria and rating scales. Performance-based evaluation allows students to demonstrate an understanding of material or concepts by applying this understanding to one or more tasks. An example of performance-based assessment in the reading classroom is using the completion of a product, such as a poster or book review, to show understanding of a trade book.

Teachers can use rubrics to assess progress in most subjects and content areas, and they can design rubrics to fit the specific needs of their classrooms. Rubrics are most effective when they are designed in collaboration with the student. In this way, the student is fully aware of the criteria that will be used for evaluation. When students are aware of expectations for a given task, they perform better.

As we know, instruction can be differentiated in terms of content, process, product, assessment, and environment. The use of rubrics can help evaluate the effectiveness of differentiated instruction in those areas. Rubrics, when designed effectively, help teachers connect instruction to authentic assessment, and thus allow students to work toward higher levels of learning. Examples of rubrics follow.

Sample Rubrics

Rubric to Assess Sequencing

4	Student is able to list in chronological order all steps and events found in the story and is able to discuss the importance of proper sequencing of a story. Student is able to synthesize key themes and how they relate to the story or outcomes. Student elaborates on details.
3	Student is able to list in chronological order most of the steps and events found in the story. Student is able to discuss the importance of proper sequencing of a story and elaborates on some details.
2	Student minimally conveys the chronological order of all steps and events found in the story. Student is not able to discuss the importance of proper sequencing of a story. Student does not include details relevant to the story.
1	Student discusses events out of order. Student often includes information that does not relate to the story, does not understand the importance of proper sequencing of a story, or provides no details.

Rubric to Assess Projects

4	Student followed all of the directions. The project is creative and neat. The student displayed a high level of knowledge related to the topic. The project has a clear purpose. The student included accurate information.
3	Student followed all of the directions. The project is creative and neat. The purpose is not as clear as expected. The student displays understanding of the topic. Most of the information is accurate.
2	Student did not follow directions. The project shows some creativity but is not neat. Information is not accurate.
1	Student turned in a project that is carelessly done and inaccurate. Project is incomplete and does not display a true understanding of the topic.
0	Student did not turn in a project as agreed upon.

Rubric to Assess Re-Tellings

4	Student re-tells the story accurately. Student includes details about events, uses important vocabulary, and organizes information effectively.
3	Student re-tells the story in an adequate manner. Student includes some details but not all, uses some vocabulary, and tries to organize information.
2	Student re-tells the story with inaccuracies. Student does not use vocabulary appropriately and cannot re-tell the story with understanding.
1	Student cannot re-tell the story accurately. Student includes information that is not in the story and does not understand the story.

Rubric to Assess Reports

	Not Yet 1	Needs Improvement 2	Satisfactory 3	Exceptional 4
Quality of Information	Information not presented	Very little information presented	Adequate details; some unrelated information is included	Complete information; lots of supporting details; all information relates to the subject
Quality of Organization	Not organized	Somewhat organized; events are not in order	Most events are well organized; very few are not in order	Clear organization; all events are in proper sequence
Grammar	Paper had a lot of grammatical errors	Paper had more than two errors	Paper had only one or two grammatical or spelling errors	Paper had no grammatical errors
Neat	Paper was not neat; writing was illegible	Writing needs improvement; letter formation not always accurate	Writing is adequate; paper is neatly bound together	Writing is excellent; paper was typed or printed in an exceptional manner; report was bound
Completion	Paper was handed in more than one week late	Paper was handed in three days late	Paper was handed in one or two days late	Paper was handed in on time

Anecdotal Records

Anecdotal records are simply teacher notes based on observations made throughout the school year. These positive narratives help document the growth and progress of students. Many teachers express concern about using anecdotal records to assess student progress and achievement because they view them as being time-consuming and subjective. They feel that they do not have time to effectively manage anecdotal records. However, anecdotal records help teachers to record the important learning moments that they notice throughout the school day and observe carefully what is happening in the classroom.

Gifted readers need to be observed in a variety of settings, including reading independently, reading aloud with the teacher, reading in a group, and reading with a partner. Teachers may also want to observe the completion of reading projects or assignments, both independently and in cooperative group settings. When keeping anecdotal records, teachers can record events and behaviors, as well as skills and attitudes. These records are a very useful way to report progress to parents during conferences.

Here are some advantages of using anecdotal records:

➤ Differentiated classrooms allow students to work at varied paces. Each student is evaluated according his or her own pace.

➤ Anecdotal records benefit students by providing documentation of their progress in a variety of different learning environments.

➤ Students who may experience anxiety often associated with traditional tests can breathe easier when they know that they are being evaluated over a longer period of time.

➤ Anecdotal records allow teachers to take notes about student progress through observations. This permits teachers to make comments that are directly related to the activity or subject being evaluated.

➤ Gifted readers benefit from this form of assessment because the notes taken by their teacher not only document student progress, but they often make suggestions for improvement as well. This does not normally happen during formal evaluations such as traditional testing.

As teachers become more comfortable using anecdotal records, they will see how this assessment tool provides them with an accurate picture of student growth. Following are some examples of anecdotal records.

Sample Anecdotal Records

Example #1

Name: Cecilia

Date: April 6, 2005

Instructional Setting: Literature discussion groups

Task: Group members are assigned four questions to discuss and answer.

Observations: C. worked well in her group – offered opinions when asked – seemed shy at times.

Future Goals: Continue giving C. opportunities to work in small groups. Try an interest survey to see how I can help her in small groups.

Example #2

Name: Jane

Date: April 6, 2005

Task: Jane is completing a project that relates to *Stay Away from Simon* by Carol Carrick. Her project requires Jane to summarize and evaluate given information.

Instructional Setting: Jane is working independently on a project outlined in a learning contract.

Observations: Jane is having trouble working independently. She frequently asks questions, as if she needs reassurance. Jane indicates that she likes to work independently.

Teacher Comments: Continue encouraging Jane to answer her own questions and set personal goals to work effectively.

Portfolio Assessment

Portfolios are collections of student works that exhibit the student's efforts, progress, and achievement. Portfolios may be assembled in file folders, shoeboxes, notebooks, or on videotapes to document student learning. Students should be allowed to create their own covers for their portfolios. Portfolios:

➤ constitute authentic evaluation.
➤ provide valid information regarding student progress because the information has been collected over extended periods of time.
➤ allow teachers to note student progress from the first of the year to the end.
➤ allow other individuals to view and evaluate progress made by students.
➤ allow gifted readers to make observations and judgments about their own progress.
➤ give gifted readers opportunities to make critical decisions.

➤ highlight student's strengths rather than weaknesses.
➤ allow a view of gifted readers as individuals and of their individual learning needs.
➤ provide positive interaction between teachers and gifted readers.

To be effective, portfolios should include these elements:

➤ clearly defined goals.
➤ samples reflecting the student's growth. These samples might include checklists, projects, anecdotal records, conference forms, peer evaluation forms, drafts of student writing, published pieces, journal articles, graphic organizers, attitude and process surveys, and evidence of student self-reflection.
➤ tasks and projects using the multiple intelligences allowing students to demonstrate understanding in various modes of instruction.
➤ a list of collaboratively developed criteria by which the portfolio will be evaluated.

Portfolio assessment is a multi-step process that allows for collaboration between teachers and students. Especially for students who learn in nontraditional ways, portfolios allow teachers to evaluate the "big picture" of students' learning. With portfolios, students have the opportunity to reflect on their own learning and to monitor and evaluate their own progress and achievement. A reading portfolio gives gifted readers opportunities to collect, select, reflect upon, and investigate their own work over time. Throughout the school year, teachers can work with students to identify significant papers, tests, and other materials to be included in the final portfolio collection.

Portfolios encourage self-directed learning and make a connection between instruction and assessment. Students who assemble portfolios understand better what is expected and learn to take responsibility for their own progress as they complete their projects and evaluate the outcomes. Portfolios also make useful tools for parent conferences. Following are some sample portfolio pages.

Sample Portfolio Pages

Table of Contents

Name:		Date:	Teacher:	
Title of Work	**Date Completed**	**Reasons for Inclusion in Portfolio**		**Page Number**

Teacher/Student Conference Form

Name:	Date:	Teacher:	
Date	**Items Discussed**	**Recommendations**	**Future Goals**

Student Self-Reflection Form

Name:	Date:	Teacher:
The thing I like best in my portfolio is:		
I need to improve:		
I have progressed in the following area(s) (list area and what improved):		
I hope these people will read and review my portfolio:		
Changes I want to make to my portfolio:		
I would like to add or remove the following items:		
What I have learned from this review:		

Peer Evaluation Form

Name:	Date:	Teacher:

Title of Work:

Name of Reviewer:

I really like the following:	**I suggest the following:**

Title of Work:

Name of Reviewer:

I really like the following:	**I suggest the following:**

Title of Work:

Name of Reviewer:

I really like the following:	**I suggest the following:**

Title of Work:

Name of Reviewer:

I really like the following:	**I suggest the following:**

Classroom Conferences

Conferences promote and provide a record of dialogue between students and teachers, and between students and other students. Students meet with teachers to discuss tasks, their feelings and attitudes about a reading assignment, or their opinions about cooperative learning projects. Students meet with peers to share feedback about projects or assignments. Students can offer advice to other students, as well as to help determine future goals.

Teachers have the flexibility to work with students one-on-one or in groups. When working in groups, teachers should take care not to discuss student grades or other private issues.

When used for assessment purposes, conferences take place before, during, or after the reading process. Teachers may establish and post a conference schedule. During scheduled times, teachers can also give students feedback on their oral reading skills. As students gain practice in meeting with their teachers, they will learn how to prepare for conferences.

Information collected at conferences should be placed in the student's portfolio as another way to document progress. Conferences have many advantages as an assessment strategy. They:

➤ provide real-time information about the student as a learner.
➤ help teachers to observe and understand which reading strategies each student uses.
➤ help students to take ownership of their own assessment.
➤ give teachers information about strengths and weaknesses displayed by gifted readers.

Following is a sample conference form.

Sample Conference Form

Teacher Note: *Use a form similar to this when students self-select a book to read independently.*

Name:_____Date: _____Teacher:_____

What is the title of the book you are reading? _____

Who is the author? _____

Have you read other books by this author? _____

Why did you choose this book? _____

What three things do you find the most interesting about this story so far? Explain why these
things are interesting to you. _____

_____

_____

_____

What do you believe is the author's purpose for writing this story? _____

_____

What impact might this story have on your beliefs or your life? Explain. _____

_____

Which characters did you relate to most and why? _____

_____

Summarize the story, sequencing the events in the proper order. _____

_____

_____

What is the main idea in this book? _____

_____

_____

Please turn to a favorite part or chapter of the book and read aloud (page ___ to page ___).

When Students Evaluate Themselves

Self-evaluation takes place when students examine and reflect on their own progress and achievements. When gifted readers evaluate themselves, they learn to take ownership of their own learning. When teachers observe students in the process of self-evaluation, they gain information about students' perceptions of their own reading. Self-evaluation promotes higher levels of learning because students learn to critically evaluate their own performances.

Students will often work more carefully when they are asked to assess their own progress. Teachers need to encourage students to self-evaluate their reading, their projects, their written responses to higher-level questions, their work samples found in portfolios, and their participation and interaction during cooperative work projects. Below are some questions that teachers can pose to students to help them evaluate their own work.

> ➤ How does your project demonstrate what you know about the topic?
> ➤ How well did you accomplish your goal? What would you have done differently?
> ➤ Identify the best things about your project.
> ➤ What areas need improvement?
> ➤ Did you use appropriate grammar?
> ➤ Does your project demonstrate creativity?
> ➤ If you could decide on your grade for this project, what would it be and why?

Teaching students to self-evaluate and complete self-evaluation forms will lead to classrooms full of goal-oriented gifted readers. Teachers may choose to have students complete checklists or narrative-style forms to document their progress. It is always beneficial to schedule meetings with gifted readers so that they may discuss their evaluations. Here are some forms to use in the self-evaluation process.

Student Self-Evaluation Form

Name:_____Date: _____Teacher:_____

Directions: Please answer each question below and give yourself a letter or number grade.

How does your project demonstrate what you know about the topic?

_____

_____

How well did you accomplish your goal? What would you have done differently?

_____

_____

Identify the best things about your project.

_____

_____

What areas need improvement? Explain.

_____

_____

Does your project demonstrate creativity? Explain.

_____

_____

Does your project reflect your best efforts? Explain.

_____

_____

What grade would you give yourself for this project? Explain why. Grade:_____

_____

_____

Comments:

_____

_____

Self-Reflection for Reading Aloud

Name:_____Date: _____Teacher:_____

Directions: Using the tape recorder in the classroom, record yourself reading several pages from your favorite part of the book.

Title of book: _____

Pages read: _____

Why did you pick this part of the story? _____

_____

As you listen to yourself reading, answer these questions:

➤ How comfortable were you with reading into the recorder? Why or why not?

_____

➤ How well do you think you did with using expression and emotions?

_____

➤ How well did you do with pronunciation? Did you read with clarity?

_____

➤ If you could re-do the recording, what would you do differently?

_____

Comments: _____

_____

_____

When Students Evaluate Each Other

Offering students opportunities to review works by peers helps to promote an environment of mutual respect among classmates. Gifted students enjoy offering advice, recommendations, and positive feedback to their peers. Many times, gifted students are able to verbalize recommendations for improvement better than we can as educators.

I remember completing a culminating activity that involved students researching a given topic and making a product that displayed their new knowledge. The students were asked to present their projects with the class. As each student presented, classmates filled out peer evaluation forms. The dialogue that was generated throughout the presentations was very respectful, informative, and heart-warming. One such interchange follows.

Student Presenter:	That completes my research and my project on the Civil War. What questions do you have?
Student 1:	Did you enjoy learning about the Civil War?
Presenter:	It was very interesting, and I especially liked learning about the conflicts in the war.
Student 2:	Where did you find most of your information?
Presenter:	I found most of it in books and online.
Student 3:	Which resource did you feel to be the most accurate?
Presenter:	I found the books to be the best source and the most reliable.
Student 4:	I thought your project was really good. I think I would have used more graphics on your poster. What do you think?
Presenter:	I see your point, but I had so much information to include, I thought I wouldn't have enough room.

These students interacted in a positive way and offered targeted feedback. The class completed peer evaluation forms for each presenter, and the students filed them in their portfolios.

Teachers can use peer evaluations for many classroom activities. Examples follow.

Cooperative Group Work

Students evaluate each other as they complete a given task.

Portfolios

The teacher assigns "portfolio partners." Students learn to give appropriate feedback through checklists and rubrics.

Presentations

Students complete evaluation forms after classmates present their projects to the class.

Projects or Displays

The teacher displays projects that the students have completed. Students walk around the room, making observations and taking notes. All students offer constructive advice and recommendations, making note of positive qualities about the projects. A sharing time is then provided.

Journal Entries

The teacher provides time for students to exchange journals. Students read entries and then complete a checklist that evaluates the quality of the journal and the entries.

Reading Partners

Students are divided into pairs. Students read aloud to each other from a trade book assigned by the teacher. Since reading aloud can be traumatic for some students, teachers should take care that it be done individually with the teacher or in very small groups for students who are uncomfortable. It should not be a part of formal assessment for such students.

Thoughts about Evaluation

Reading development varies depending on students' academic, personal, social, and cultural needs. Gifted readers have specific needs that must be met within the regular classroom. Just as teachers implement a variety of instructional strategies to meet these needs, they must also use a variety of assessment strategies. These include assessing reading abilities and attitudes through the use of checklists, rubrics, anecdotal records, portfolios, and conferences, along with the usual projects and tests. Teachers may also choose to provide opportunities for students to assess themselves and each other. Variety in instruction and assessment promotes an environment that fosters higher levels of learning.

Assessment Strategies Overview

Strategy	Description	Benefits
Pre-Assessment	Teachers test students on given material to see if material has already been mastered	➤ Helps eliminate unnecessary work for students ➤ Allows students to move forward in their learning. ➤ Facilitates the practice of grouping students by abilities
Checklists	A tool to help teachers evaluate students by "checking off" certain behaviors, skills, or performances	➤ Can be used along with other types of assessment ➤ Can be used randomly and throughout the year ➤ Provide reliable information without taking too much time
Rubrics	A form of performance-based evaluation that requires students to demonstrate their understanding of material or concepts by using specific criteria and rating scales	➤ Help evaluate the process of differentiating instruction ➤ Make students aware of expectations before completing projects
Anecdotal Records	Narratives conducted by the teacher to help document the growth and progress of students, i.e., teacher notes based on observations	➤ Allow students to work at an individual pace because teachers are evaluating them on their individual performances ➤ Provide teachers with valid feedback because the information has been collected throughout the year ➤ Encourages teachers to make future goals with students based on the information received
Portfolios	Collections of student works that display the efforts and progress of the student; can be collected in binders, boxes, or even on videotape	➤ Highlight student strengths ➤ Provide long-term data regarding student progress ➤ Allow for others to get involved in the assessment process ➤ Give students opportunities to analyze and make judgments about their learning

Strategy	Description	Benefits
Conferences	Discussions take place about student attitudes toward reading assignments, opinions, and cooperative learning projects; provide a record of dialogue between students and teachers, and students and students	➤ Information collected can be placed in portfolios ➤ Provide real-time information about the student as a learner ➤ Help teachers understand reading strategies used by the students ➤ Help students take ownership of their own assessment ➤ Provide verbal students opportunities to express themselves with the teacher
Self-Reflection	Opportunities to reflect on one's own progress and growth through careful examination of work	➤ Promotes higher levels of thinking because students learn to critically evaluate their own performances ➤ Encourages students to take more responsibility in their learning
Peer Evaluation	Opportunities to review work by peers	➤ Promotes an environment of mutual respect among classmates ➤ Can be used in a variety of settings and for a variety of subjects ➤ Shows students that teachers care about their opinions

Key Points

✎ Assessment is needed to measure student growth.

✎ Teachers must use a variety of assessment strategies, as well as a variety of teaching strategies, to meet the needs of different students.

✎ Teachers can evaluate students, or students can evaluate themselves.

✎ Pre-assessment is needed to determine reading levels.

✎ Checklists are useful for quick assessment.

✎ Rubrics listing expectations for a task can be designed collaboratively with the student.

✎ Anecdotal records based on observations can be made throughout the school year.

✎ Portfolios can document growth and progress over time.

✎ Classroom conferences promote dialog between teachers and students and provide real-time information.

✎ Students who evaluate themselves learn to take ownership of their learning.

Chapter 8
Communicating about Reading

Communication: The exchange of thoughts, messages, or the like, by speech, signals, or writing. A system for sending and receiving messages.
—*The American Heritage Dictionary*

Communication

Open and frequent communication between teachers, students, and parents is an important part of any reading program, even for gifted readers. Communication opens doors for parents to become a part of their child's education. Parents appreciate having teachers inform them about the reading curriculum and strategies that will be used in the classroom.

Communication comes in many forms, both written and oral. It may include newsletters, phone calls, conferences, notes sent home, invitations to observe, reading nights, and support groups. When teachers are comfortable with these means of communication, they realize the importance of providing regular information to parents.

> I met with a new teacher who was getting many questions from parents. She had three students in her class reading at advanced levels. This young teacher was doing everything right. She was compacting her curriculum, offering opportunities to pre-test out of the basal reading text, offering trade books to these students, and differentiating her reading curriculum in a variety of ways. However, the parents did not see these strategies taking place. They continued to call and ask what was taking place in reading to help meet the needs of their children. I suggested that she add a section in her classroom newsletter that would identify the differentiated reading strategies that she was using. The teacher additionally decided to provide definitions for many of the terms used in the newsletter, for example, "curriculum compacting." The following week, this young and enthusiastic teacher wrote this in her newsletter:

We continue to make great progress in reading. This week, many students participated in enrichment centers after pre-testing out of the regular reading curriculum. The students are enjoying reading trade books that have been chosen based on their individual ability levels. All students have the opportunity to take the pre-test.

After sending this newsletter home, the teacher received several notes from parents. They expressed their appreciation for the informative newsletter and said that they'd had no idea that these strategies were being used with their children.

Sometimes it just takes a few sentences for teachers to let parents know what a great job they do in their classrooms. Teachers, don't be afraid to blow your own horn now and then! You work too hard to keep your successes to yourself.

Newsletters

Newsletters are one of the most effective ways of communicating with parents and students. Newsletters sent on a regular basis:

➤ provide information about what the children are learning and what instructional strategies are being used.
➤ help parents and students feel a part of the learning team.
➤ inform parents of upcoming stories and themes.
➤ educate them about differentiated reading programs.
➤ accentuate the positive attitudes in the classroom.
➤ incorporate and highlight students' work.

Some suggestions to create a classroom newsletter:

➤ Let the students create the name and logo of the newsletter, giving it instant recognition when it arrives home.
➤ Allow students to contribute to the contents of each issue of the newsletter and help to publish it.
➤ The newsletter should appear on a regular basis so that parents know when to check their children's backpacks.
➤ Include information that relates to stories that you have read and will be reading.
➤ Include a section that offers ideas and tips for promoting reading at home.
➤ Keep the writing informal and friendly. Do not include too many technical terms.
➤ Define terms such as "learning contract," "curriculum compacting," and "activity menus."
➤ Include a calendar of due dates for projects.
➤ Distribute the newsletters to parents, administrators, and team members.

Sample Parent Newsletter

The Communicator

2nd Grade   Mrs. McWilliams   Room 5

The students continue to make great progress as we explore different topics in our classroom. We just read a variety of trade books that were chosen based on the needs of all students. The students really enjoyed the time spent reading independently, as well as in small groups. After reading, the students completed projects that they chose based on their individual interests. Some students displayed their knowledge gained by creating posters, while others chose to perform skits.

We would love to share some of the great things that we have been doing in our classroom. The students continue to work on the process of evaluating their own work progress through the use of portfolios. If you would like to come in and observe our differentiated reading program in progress, please let us know.

Reading Grams or Literature Loops

Reading grams and literature loops are easy! A short note written by the teacher to the parent gives parents a quick update of progress. The parent then returns the note to the teacher with a signature or any questions, thus making a loop back to the teacher.

Sample Reading Gram or Literature Loop

Dear Mrs. Marshall,   August 7, 2005

This is just a quick note to let you know that Katelyn has completed the story *Stay Away from Simon* by Carol Carrick. In the next couple of weeks, Katelyn will be completing three projects that relate to this story.

Because Katelyn demonstrated an understanding of the story that was in the basal and the skills associated with it, these projects will take the place of the work that she would have been expected to do with the basal story. Please ask her to tell you about *Stay Away from Simon* and the other projects that she is working on. If you have any questions for me, please write them below.

Parent Comments/Questions:

Signature of Parent: _____Date: _____

Parent Conferences

Phone conferences or conferences at school can be useful tools that teachers can use for communicating with parents.

Phone Conferences

Because today's busy schedules often make it hard for parents to come to their child's school, phone conferences may be used to communicate with parents about their child's reading. The following suggestions will help to make phone conferences effective, efficient, and enjoyable:

➤ Keep track of phone conferences, and record parent comments on index cards.
➤ Keep calls brief.
➤ Make positive phone calls on a regular basis.
➤ If you have a concern, remember to stay focused, state the problem, and include suggestions.

Conferences at School

Conferences that take place at school between parents and teachers are extremely effective when they are carefully planned. Because a differentiated reading program does not typically follow the same pattern of instruction as other classroom activities, ongoing communication is crucial in order to keep parents informed about reading instruction and to report progress made by students. For example, a differentiated reading program involves multiple instructional strategies taking place simultaneously, while reading programs that use a basal reading text often use only one instructional strategy and do not promote flexibility within the program. A differentiated reading program allows teachers to be flexible so that they can better meet the needs of individual students. The integration of trade books into a differentiated reading program allows teachers to use learning contracts, reading activity menus, and literature discussion groups. Because the strategies used in differentiated reading instruction are not typically used in most reading programs, parents often have questions for teachers. Conferences help teachers to answer these questions and provide information about the differentiated reading program.

The following suggestions to plan and conduct conferences will benefit parents, students, and teachers:

➤ Prepare a list of items to share with the parents. Decide what is important to reinforce. Be organized. Ask yourself, "What do I want the parent to know after the conference?"
➤ Make parents feel welcome and not defensive.
➤ Share samples of student work.
➤ Share copies of learning contracts and activity menus.
➤ Show parents a schedule of a typical day in reading.
➤ Share a copy of the student's journal.
➤ Keep focused. Keep your comments friendly but brief. Try not to get off track.
➤ Ask parents how they feel about the reading program. Ask them if they feel that their child is succeeding in reading.
➤ Conclude conferences by restating points and issues.
➤ Keep a log of all conferences.

Reading Passes

Reading passes are invitations that teachers send to principals, teachers from previous years, school board members, community members, grandparents, parents, and others to invite them to come and observe what happens in the reading classroom. Reading passes promote reading programs. When visitors see differentiation or compacting in action in the classroom, they are more likely to be supportive of the program. When students have visitors in the classroom, they are motivated to work harder. When community members and board members understand what is meant by differentiation, they will be more supportive of funding for materials needed for these programs. Here is how to begin using reading passes:

➤ Decide how frequently you will issue reading passes. Letting observers into the classroom twice a month is usually not too intrusive to classroom management.

➤ Involve students in the planning. Ask them what reading activities they would like to take place while observers are in the classroom, and have them help write this information on the reading passes.

➤ Set up reading stations to allow visitors to see multiple learning strategies.

➤ Decide the visitors' role ahead of time. Will visitors strictly observe, or will they take part in the activities?

Sample Invitation to Observe

Dear _____,

What is a *learning contract*? What is a *reading activity menu*? What is meant by *curriculum compacting*? What is a *rubric*?

If you would like to know the answers to these and other questions, please come to our classroom for a half-hour visit on _____ at _____. You will have the chance to learn about these exciting reading strategies while you observe our class during reading time. We are very excited about the progress that we continue to make in reading and would love to share this excitement with you!

Please RSVP to _____Phone: _____

Sincerely,
Your friends in _____ classroom

Reading Nights

Organize a special reading night when parents can come into the classroom and take part in various reading activities. The teacher may wish to demonstrate how curriculum compacting works in the classroom. Students may invite their parents to ask questions about the program or to participate in a literature discussion group. Parents may actually complete a learning contract or an activity menu. Include school administrators along with the parents.

Reading Volunteers

In addition to reading nights, many schools hold a "Back to School Night" at the beginning of the year. Both of these events provide the perfect opportunity to ask for family or community members to volunteer as "reading partners."

Reading partners offer some of their time to work with students in reading instruction. When reading partners are available, the classroom teacher works with small groups of students who are together based on their ability. The volunteer works with other students, using materials such as trade books, journals, and graphic organizers. The reading volunteer may listen to students read, hold brief discussions about the story, and then work with students on an extension project.

This strategy works well with all students. Parents and community members appreciate the opportunity to get involved in their children's educations. Students enjoy the time spent with adults. Teachers benefit because it provides them with much needed time to work with small groups of gifted readers, as well as with students who need extra reinforcement.

Surveys, Questionnaires, Inventories

Surveys, questionnaires, and inventories provide teachers with valuable information about students' needs, attitudes, and interests. Administering an interest survey or inventory at various times throughout the school year allows teachers to use the information in future lesson plans and classroom activities. For example, if students express an interest in a given area or theme, teachers can make a point of choosing trade books that relate to that theme. Teachers can use questionnaires to poll students after they have read a book. These questionnaires help the teacher determine whether students liked the book and whether reading it was worthwhile.

Surveys, questionnaires, and inventories can also be given to parents. Teachers may wish to use this form of communication to gather information about parents' expectations for successful reading programs. As parents complete the forms, they will realize that a partnership exists between school and home. Effective communication ensures that all parties involved are aware of expectations and goals. Everyone involved—students, teachers, parents, and administrators—is invited to give input as to what they would like to see happen in the classroom. The use of surveys, questionnaires, and inventories can help all parties to feel comfortable expressing themselves.

The following are examples of surveys, questionnaires, and inventories that have proven useful in the classroom.

Teacher Survey

	Sometimes	Yes	No
1. I feel comfortable differentiating reading instruction.	❏	❏	❏
2. I use pre-testing as a way of moving students forward in reading.	❏	❏	❏
3. I believe that a reading program works best when a basal reading series is used independently.	❏	❏	❏
4. I feel comfortable identifying gifted readers.	❏	❏	❏
5. I use alternate assessment tools in my class.	❏	❏	❏
6. I typically use whole-class instruction instead of group work.	❏	❏	❏
7. I allow students to make choices based on their interests.	❏	❏	❏
8. I would like to learn more strategies to help meet the needs of gifted readers.	❏	❏	❏
9. I feel comfortable choosing trade books for gifted readers.	❏	❏	❏
10. I often use a variety of instructional strategies for all students.	❏	❏	❏

Student Interest Survey

Name:_____Date: _____Teacher:_____

1. Why do you think that it is important for your teacher to get to know you?

_____

_____

2. Do you like school? Rate this year by giving it a number from 1 to 10 (where 10 is the best).

_____

_____

3. What is your favorite subject in school?

_____

4. Are there any subjects in school that are difficult for you?

_____

_____

5. Do you like to read? What types of books do you like to read?

_____

_____

6. List three things that you like to do after school.

_____

_____

_____

7. Do you like working on projects in school by yourself or in a small group?

_____

_____

8. Do you participate in sports? If so, which ones?

_____

_____

9. If you could make any subject in school longer, which would it be and why?

_____

_____

10. Do you have a hobby? If so, tell about it.

_____

_____

_____

11. Do you collect any items of interest? Tell about this collection.

_____

_____

_____

12. You have been asked by your teacher to plan the next field trip. Where would you choose to go and why?

_____

_____

_____

13. Describe your ideal school day.

_____

_____

_____

14. Is there anything that you feel your teacher needs to know about you?

_____

_____

_____

15. Do you have a lot of friends at school? At home?

_____

_____

_____

Is there anything else that you would like to share?

_____

_____

_____

_____

Parent Survey

Child's Name:_____Date: _____Teacher:_____

Dear Parents/Guardians,

In an effort to better meet the needs of your child, I am gathering information that will help me create a more positive learning environment. Please complete the form below so that I can help your child be successful at school.

	No	Sometimes	Yes
Enjoys working with peers on a group project			
Reads independently at home			
Likes to have goals established			
Enjoys school			
Likes to work independently on school assignments			
Is comfortable with most subjects at school			
Participates in sports			
Has many friends at school			
Has many friends at home			
Enjoys listening to music			
Is tolerant of other students			
Can work on projects for long periods of time			
Uses advanced vocabulary			
Does not like conflict			
Enjoys art activities			
Would rather work with hands to show knowledge about a topic (i.e., a poster)			
Is very competitive			
If unsure, will ask for help			
Enjoys helping others			

Possible concerns (check all that apply):

❏ Is a perfectionist; often gets upset if something is not perfect

❏ Is unorganized

❏ Seems bored in school

❏ Talks negatively about school

❏ Talks about being different from peers

Parent Questionnaire

Child's Name:_____Date: _____Teacher:_____

Dear Parents/Guardians:

In an effort to better meet the needs of gifted readers at _____ (name of school), we are asking parents to complete this questionnaire. The information will be reviewed by a committee at our school and used to determine the effectiveness of our reading program for gifted or advanced readers. Your feedback will help us design reading instruction that enables our students to move forward in their learning. Please complete the questionnaire and send it back to school with your child or place it in the box in our office.

Grade level of your child _____   Male or female _____

1. Does your child speak positively about reading instruction at school?
   If not, what concerns does your child have regarding reading?

   _____

   _____

2. Briefly describe the reading program that your child is currently in at school.

   _____

   _____

3. Does your child read at home?

   _____

   _____

4. List the types of books that your child likes to read.

   _____

   _____

5. Do you feel that your child's needs are met in reading at school?
   If not, what would you suggest?

   _____

   _____

6. Do you feel that your child has adjusted well at school this year? Explain.

   _____

   _____

7. Does your child enjoy coming to school each day?

_____

_____

8. Would you be interested in attending an evening workshop for parents that
   demonstrates differentiated reading strategies that we currently use at our school?

_____

_____

9. Does your child prefer to work in small groups or alone?

_____

_____

10. What does your child like to do after school?

_____

_____

11. We believe that our school has an outstanding reading program. However, we feel that
    there is always room for improvement. What suggestions would you make to help
    us improve our reading program for gifted readers?

_____

_____

_____

_____

Thank you for taking the time to complete this questionnaire.

Administrator Self-Reflection Inventory

This form may be used to help administrators and other leaders think about reading programs.

1. Approximately how many students are identified as gifted in your school?

   _____

2. Do you think that your teachers are comfortable providing instruction for gifted readers?

   _____

3. Does your school offer opportunities for teachers and support staff to learn more about identifying gifted readers?

   _____

4. Are you interested in holding an in-service for teachers that offers instructional strategies for gifted readers?

   _____

5. Do your teachers have a positive attitude about gifted students?

   _____

6. What resources can you offer for providing your staff with information about gifted readers?

   _____

7. Do your feel that your staff is comfortable coming to you with concerns they might have?

   _____

8. Do you feel that your school is currently doing everything it can to help gifted readers reach their full potential?

   _____

9. Do your teachers have supplies and materials needed to effectively teach gifted students?

   _____

10. How do you communicate your successes in reading with parents? How might this change?

    _____

Teacher Exchange Board

A teacher exchange board is an excellent way to encourage teacher-to-teacher communication about reading. A decorative bulletin board placed in the teachers' lounge can invite teachers to share information about instructional strategies that work well with gifted readers. Teachers might post examples of activity menus that have been effective, or they might share ideas about curriculum compacting or learning contracts. As teachers eat lunch, they can read the suggestions and discuss them with their colleagues.

The teacher exchange board is also a good place to post current articles that relate to reading instruction, especially for gifted students. By keeping abreast of current research, teachers can more easily create and maintain effective reading programs.

Here are suggestions for creating a teacher exchange board in your school:

➤ Decide on a central location.
➤ Decorate the bulletin board to make it appealing. Teachers may want to take turns doing this by month or quarter.
➤ During a faculty meeting, explain the use of the board, and invite all teachers to use it to share ideas and strategies or to post questions and needs. Suggest that they post samples of learning contracts, activity menus, management techniques, titles of books, assessment strategies, graphic organizers, examples of higher-level questions, and communication tools that they use in the classroom.
➤ Use forms that are accessible and easy to fill out (see the following example).
➤ Survey staff frequently to see if the bulletin board is effective.

Sample Forms for Teacher Exchange Boards

Guess What Works for Me!

| Teacher Name:_____Date: _____ |

Idea or strategy to share:

_____

_____

_____

_____

Any Ideas?

I need ideas for a group of gifted readers who continue to ask for challenging material. Any ideas you have to offer would be greatly appreciated. If you have an idea, please stop by to see me or place a note in my box. Thank you!

Thoughts about Communication

Good communication benefits students, teachers, parents, and the community. The better students understand the reading program, the more they will strive to succeed. Accordingly, the better parents and administrators understand the reading program, the more supportive they will be. Teachers can use a variety of strategies to help parents, students, and administrators understand the many parts of a reading program, including goals, expectations, procedures, instructional strategies, and assessment tools.

Don't keep success and hard work in the classroom a secret. Communicate!

Key Points

Parents appreciate receiving information about the reading program.

✎ Newsletters provide information and help parents feel involved.

✎ Reading grams from the teacher give parents a quick update on their child's progress.

✎ Parent conferences are most effective when planned in advance.

✎ Reading passes can be issued to invite community members to the school to observe.

✎ Reading partners are parents or other volunteers who come in to the classroom to help children with their reading.

✎ Questionnaires and surveys are useful to determine a child's special reading interests.

✎ A teacher survey can indicate additional skills that teachers need.

✎ A parent survey may offer helpful information about a child's attitude toward reading.

✎ Teachers may enjoy sharing ideas and activities through a teacher exchange board.

Chapter 9
Final Thoughts

Because gifted students are often able to read by the time they enter school, their reading instruction may need to be individualized to maintain their enthusiasm. Students who have mastered the basics of reading might be permitted to use literature in place of basal readers.
—Kenneth Shore

In my years as a teacher, I have witnessed many changes in education. Times change, but one thing has remained the same: the needs of gifted readers. They still need—and will always need—reading materials that spark their interest and move their academic progress forward.

Gifted readers may become "stale" when they are not provided with challenging materials. It is not appropriate to limit them to the basal reading text. This form of instruction is not very effective with them.

With this in mind, we should commit to modify our reading programs to meet the needs of gifted readers. Change is never easy. Routines become reliable and comfortable. We tend to keep these routines around for long periods of time—often far too long.

Consider the following guidelines for change:

➤ Treat all students equally, taking into account their learning needs and abilities.
➤ Start adapting your curriculum slowly. Try one or two new strategies that help differentiate reading instruction for gifted readers. When you become comfortable with those, try more.
➤ Group gifted readers together so that they may interact with their intellectual peers.
➤ Provide gifted readers with opportunities to participate in small group and independent projects that allow them to solve real problems. Basal reading texts often fail to provide this type of learning.
➤ Teach gifted readers a series of reading strategies instead of isolated reading skills.
➤ Provide trade books containing gifted characters, sophisticated vocabulary, complex story lines, and themes of interest to gifted students.
➤ Move away from traditional assessment procedures. Try using portfolios and rubrics to assess progress made by gifted readers.
➤ Communicate, communicate, communicate! Keep parents and administrators informed of the many exciting things taking place in your classroom.

The Gifted Readers' Bill of Rights
According to Bertie Kingore

Gifted readers have the right:

➤ to read at a pace and level appropriate to readiness without regard to grade placement.

➤ to discuss issues, insights, and interpretation with intellectual peers.

➤ to reread many books and not finish every book.

➤ to use reading to explore new and challenging information and grow intellectually.

➤ to have time to pursue a self-selected topic in depth through reading and writing.

➤ to encounter and apply increasingly advanced vocabulary, word study, and concepts.

➤ to guidance rather than dictation of what is good literature and how to find the best.

➤ to read several books at the same time.

➤ to discuss but not to have to defend reading choice or taste.

➤ to be excused from material already mastered (Kingore, 2002a, p. 11).

To improve is to change; to be perfect is to change often.
—Winston Churchill

Change starts when one sees the next step.
—William Drayton

Gifted readers have the right to receive instruction that makes their education a success.

Are you ready for change?

Appendix

Tools of the Trade: Reproducible Templates and Forms

The forms that are found in this section are included to help make differentiation more effective for teachers. You will find such things as learning contracts, activity menus, graphic organizers, and blank journal pages. These tools are explained in Chapters 3 and 4.

Templates and forms are reproducible. Teachers should feel free to adapt these pages to meet the needs of their students. Journal pages may be reproduced multiple times in order to make complete journals for students.

A Quick Reference Guide to Differentiation

Strategies:	Comments:
1) Learning Contracts	What have you used?
2) Permission to Read Ahead	
3) Curriculum Compacting	
4) Questioning	
5) Literature Discussion Groups	
6) Journals	
a) Free-Write	
b) Reflective and Response	
c) Multiple Entry	
d) Illustration	
e) Critical Thinking	
f) Synthesis	
g) Quotation	
h) Comprehensive	
i) Prediction	
7) Flexible Grouping	What works best?
8) Tiered Assignments	
9) Learning Centers	
10) Literature Binders	
11) Role Playing	
12) Reading Buddies	
13) Classroom Reading Box	
14) Activity Menus	
15) Read, Rotate, Record	
16) Graphic Organizers	
a) Chain of Events	
b) Storyboards	
c) Clustering	
d) Problem/Solution	
e) Venn-Diagram	
f) Spider Map	

Student Learning Contract

Name:_____Date: _____Teacher:_____

Alternative Activities (List at least five activities):

1. _____

2. _____

3. _____

4. _____

5. _____

I will complete activities #_____ and #_____ that are listed above. I will complete the activities on my own and turn completed projects into the teacher on _____

Supplies I will need for the activities: _____

_____

I have another idea for an activity or project. (*Write you idea below and have it approved by your teacher.*) _____

_____

Working conditions *(To be completed by the teacher)*: _____

_____

I will ask for help by writing a note to my teacher. I will not disturb others as I work independently.

_____   _____
Teacher's Signature   Date   Student's Signature   Date

Literature Discussion Groups

1. Members in the group: _____

_____

_____

2. Book that will be discussed: _____

Author: _____

3. Sample questions to help promote effective discussions:

   ➤ What lessons are learned in this story?

   ➤ Could this story have taken place in a different setting?

   ➤ If you could change the ending, what would it be?

   ➤ If you were the author, how would you write a sequel?

   ➤ Could any of the characters be eliminated from the story? Tell which and why.

   ➤ Are there parts to the story that teach us about perseverance?

   ➤ If you could change the behaviors of one of the characters, which character would it be and why?

   ➤ Have you ever read a story similar to this one? Tell about it.

   ➤ What was you favorite part?

   ➤ Were there any quotes that you feel made the story more powerful?

   ➤ What genre is this story?

   ➤ Can your group retell the story so that others may learn about it?

   ➤ Why do you believe that the author wrote this story?

4. Use a separate sheet of paper to write questions and answers that your group discussed.

5. Did everyone participate in the group? _____

Reading Activity Menu

Name:_____Date: _____Teacher:_____

Directions: Choose three of the activities listed below to do in place of your regular assignments. You will work on these projects during times designated by your teacher. Record dates for which you work, as well as any notes about the projects selected.

Dates: **Activity:**

_____   _____

_____   _____

_____   _____

_____   _____

_____   _____

You may also choose to create your own three activities to complete. Write your ideas below and share them with your teacher. Think about areas that interest you.

1. _____

2. _____

3. _____

Student Comments:_____

_____

Teacher Comments: _____

_____

Graphic Organizer
Chain of Events

Name:_____Date: _____Teacher:_____

Title of Book: _____

Author: _____

Directions: Complete the graphic organizer below using information from the story.

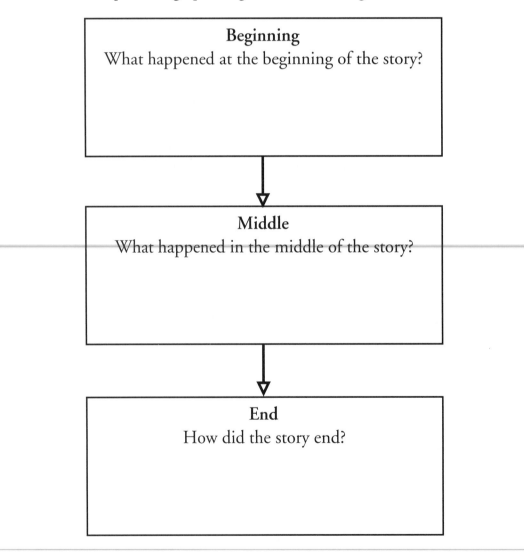

Beginning
What happened at the beginning of the story?

Middle
What happened in the middle of the story?

End
How did the story end?

Graphic Organizer
Storyboard

Name:_____ Date: _____ Teacher:_____

Title of Book: _____

Author: _____

Directions: Complete the storyboard below by recalling events from the story that you read.

Graphic Organizer
Clustering

Name:_____Date: _____Teacher:_____

Title of Book: _____

Author: _____

Directions: Fill in this graphic organizer according to the assignment.

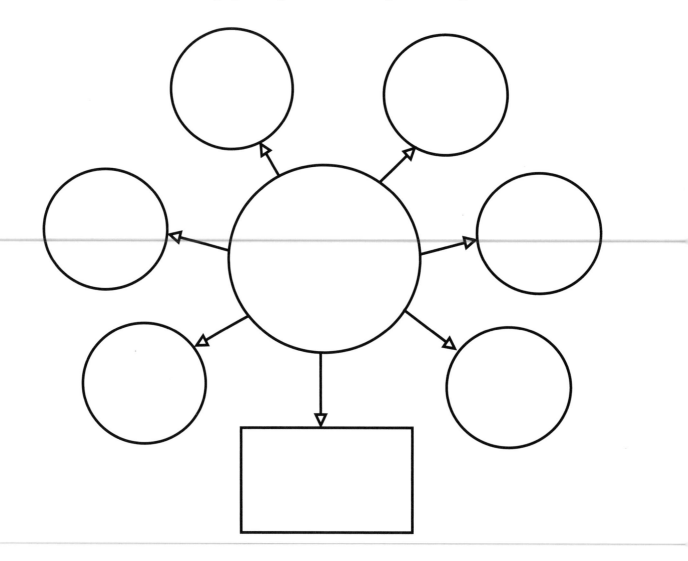

Graphic Organizer
Problem/Solution

Name:_____Date: _____Teacher:_____

Title of Book: _____

Author: _____

Directions: Complete the graphic organizer below using information from the story that you read.

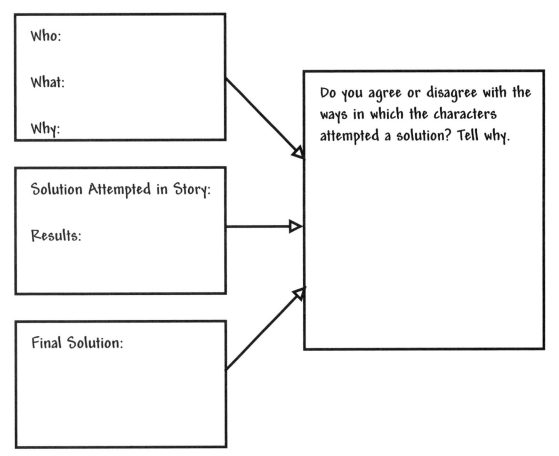

Who:

What:

Why:

Solution Attempted in Story:

Results:

Final Solution:

Do you agree or disagree with the ways in which the characters attempted a solution? Tell why.

Graphic Organizer
Venn-Diagram

Name:_____Date: _____Teacher:_____

Title of Book: _____

Author: _____

Directions: Use the Venn-diagram below to help you compare and contrast information from the story.

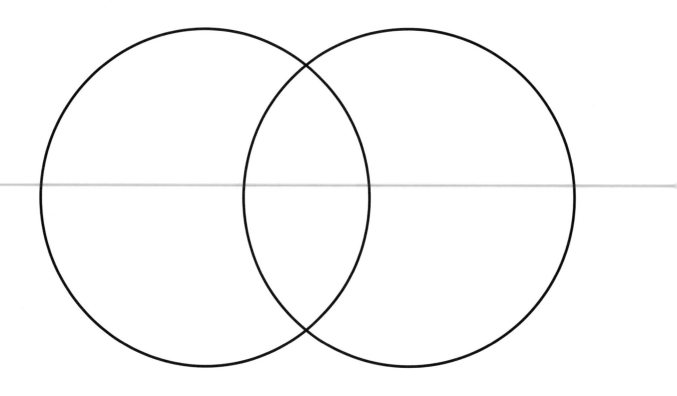

Graphic Organizer
Spider Map

Name:_____Date: _____Teacher:_____

Title of Book: _____

Author: _____

Directions: Using information from the story, describe the central ideas and their importance to the story.

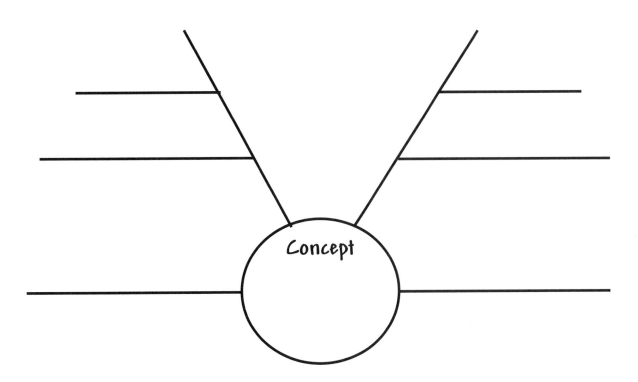

Journal Entry
Reflective and Response

Reflective and Response Journal		
What happened?	How did I feel?	What did I learn?

Journal Entry
Multiple Entry

Multiple Entry Journal		
Quotation or Character's Actions	My Thoughts	Character's Name

Journal Entry
Illustration

Illustration Journal	
Sequence of Events	Illustrations
1.	
2.	
3.	
4.	
5.	

Journal Entry
Synthesis

Synthesis Journal		
What I did	**What I learned**	**How can I use it?**

Journal Entry
Quotation

Directions: As you read your book, write down quotations that you find interesting or powerful to the story. Think about the quotation and what it means. Then decide why the quotation is important.

Quotation Journal			
Quotation	page #	What I think it means	Why is it important?

Journal Entry
Prediction

Prediction Journal		
I am on page number:	I predict this will happen:	What actually happened?

Teacher/Student Conference Form

Name:_____Date: _____Teacher:_____

Book being discussed: _____

Author: _____

Date started reading book: _____Expected date to finish book: _____

Why do you believe that the author chose to write this book?

Have there been any parts of the story that you do not understand?

Do you think that the author could restate the problem in a different way? If so, how?

Do you like this story? Why or why not?

What is your opinion of the story?

Can you tell me something about the plot?

Is there anything in this story that relates to your life?

Has anything happened in the story that changes your beliefs about given issues? Explain.

Who are the main characters in your book?

Does the story make sense to you?

What genre is your book?

Would you recommend this book to a friend? Why or why not?

Are there any parts of the story that upset you?

Other questions or comments:

Reading Buddies

Directions: Give this form to reading buddies so that they may begin. This sheet provides a focus for optimum learning and record keeping, as well as ideas on how to handle students' time together.

Ideas for Reading Buddies

- ➤ Name your team.
- ➤ Read passages together.
- ➤ Share your thoughts about the story.
- ➤ Make a list of questions your group may have.
- ➤ Make predictions about the story.
- ➤ Talk about quotes found in the story.
- ➤ Talk about characters and their actions.
- ➤ Identify the plot of the story.
- ➤ Sit and read quietly and then discuss what you both read.
- ➤ Talk about the illustrations and how they add to the story.
- ➤ Discuss the importance of the title of the book.
- ➤ Create a new beginning for your story.
- ➤ Choose a team logo and make a picture of the logo.
- ➤ Take notes during your meeting and then report back to the whole class or your teacher.
- ➤ Retell the story in the correct order.
- ➤ Decide what you will discuss during your next meeting.

Briefly record what your group talked about:

_____

_____

_____

_____

Choice Menu

This tool helps students as they choose activities and projects that they would like to complete. This is an excellent way to differentiate instruction based on student interest.

1.	2.
➤ Pick a part in the story (a passage or a scene). Write a paragraph describing this event and then provide an illustration. ➤ Locate 10 verbs, 10 nouns, and 10 adjectives in the story. Write these words on a sheet of paper. ➤ Write a short paragraph that describes the main character. What does he or she look like? How does he or she act?	➤ Create a word search using 10 words from the story. Be sure you include an answer key. ➤ Pretend that your book has become a TV show. Create an ad for the show that would appear in the TV guide. ➤ Locate five compound words, and write them in sentences.
3.	**4.**
➤ Write a conversation between you and one of the characters in the story. ➤ Create a board game that relates to the book you read. ➤ Decide if this book is one that you would like to recommend to a friend. Write a paragraph that tells your opinion of the book. Give examples to help convince your friend.	➤ Create a cartoon that describes two characters in the book. ➤ Divide a sheet of construction paper into three sections. Section 1: Draw a picture that tells about the beginning of the story. Section 2: Draw a picture that tells about the middle of the story. Section 3: Draw a picture that tells about the end of the story. ➤ Write a paragraph that tells five things you learned while reading your book.

Skills Matrix

This matrix can be used to reinforce a variety of skills. As you are teaching given skills in your basal reading text, use a skills matrix to help differentiate your instruction. The students may choose a box to complete, or the teacher may assign a box to the students. This matrix works the same as the tic-tac-toe menu in Chapter 5. Feel free to add more boxes, and then encourage the students to get three in a row.

Locate a paragraph from the book. Rewrite that paragraph, making grammatical errors. Give your paper to a friend. That friend must correct your paragraph so that it is grammatically correct.	Look through the book. Locate words in the story that have short vowel letters. Make a chart on a sheet of paper to show your words. a e i o u	Locate 10 verbs or action words in the story. Write a sentence for each word. Underline the action word.
ABRACADABRA! Change or add endings to words to make new words. Find words in the story that end in "e" and then change them to "ing," "ed," "er," "est," or "y" to make new words. For example: Come – coming	Examine the story carefully. Locate an example of a/an: ➤ Exclamatory sentence. ➤ Derogatory sentence. ➤ Imperative sentence. Write your sentences on a sheet of paper and tell what type of sentences they are.	Words such as "big," "tiny," and "fast" are called describing words. Locate words in the story that tell readers more about the characters because they are describing words. Write the words that you locate on a sheet of paper and then put them into sentences.

References

Bloom, B. (1956). *A taxonomy of educational objectives. Handbook 1.* New York: McKay.

Butler, A., & Turbil, J. (1987). *Towards a reading and writing classroom.* Portsmouth, NH: Heinemann.

Clark, B. (1983). *Growing up gifted: Developing the potential of children at home and at school* (2nd ed). Columbus, OH: Merrill.

Clark, B. (2002). *Growing up gifted: Developing the potential of children at home and at school* (6th ed.). Columbus, OH: Merrill Prentice Hall.

Collins, N., & Aiex, N. (1995). *Gifted readers and reading instruction.* ERIC (ED 3796370). Bloomington, IN: Clearinghouse on Reading, English, and Communication.

Gardner, H. (1983). *Frames of the mind: The theory of multiple intelligences.* New York: Basic Books.

Gunning, T. (1992). *Creative reading instruction for all children.* Boston: Allyn & Bacon.

Halsted, J. (1990). *Guiding the gifted reader.* ERIC (ED 321486). Arlington, VA: Clearinghouse on Handicapped and Gifted Children.

Halsted, J. W. (2002). *Some of my best friends are books, 2nd ed. guiding gifted readers from preschool to high school.* Scottsdale, AZ: Great Potential Press.

Heacox, D. (2002). *Differentiating instruction in the regular classroom.* Minneapolis, MN: Free Spirit.

Kanevsky, L. (1999). *The tool kit for curriculum differentiation.* Burnaby, BC: Simon Fraser University.

Kingore, B. (2001). Gifted kids, gifted characters, and great books. *Gifted Child Today, 24,* 30-32.

Kingore, B. (2002a). *Reading instruction for the primary gifted learner.* Retrieved September 3, 2003, from www.bertiekingore.com/readinginstruction.htm.

Kingore, B. (2002b). *Reading strategies for advanced readers.* Austin: TX: Educational Agency.

Larkin, M. (1997). Graphic organizers. *The Collaborator, 5(2).* (A publication of the Resource/Collaborative Teaching Masters in Education Program at the College of William and Mary.).

Mason, J., & Au, K. (1990). *Reading instruction for today.* New York: Harper Collins.

Merkley, D., & Jefferies, D. (2001). Guidelines for implementing graphic organizers. *The Reading Teacher, 54,* 350-357.

Painter, J. (1996). *Questioning strategies for gifted students.* Retrieved July 23, 2003, from www.nexus.edu.au/teachstud/gat/painter.htm.

Renzulli, J. S. (1977). *Interest-a-lyzer.* Mansfield Center, CT: Creative Learning Press.

Reis, S., Gubbins, E., & Richards, S. (2002) *Meeting the needs of talented readers: SEM-R.* Retrieved November 27, 2002, from www.sp.uconn.edu/%7Enrcgt/reis/readers.pdf.

Richards, S. (2002). *Books as hooks for grabbing gifted readers.* Storrs, CT: National Research Center on the Gifted and Talented, University of Connecticut.

Rogers, K. B. (2002a). *Re-forming gifted education: How parents and teachers can match the program to the child.* Scottsdale, AZ: Great Potential Press.

Rogers, K. B. (2002b). *The gifted education planner: Inventories and data collection forms.* Scottsdale, AZ: Great Potential Press.

Sakiey, E. (1980). *Reading for the gifted.* ERIC (ED 186881). Arlington, VA: Clearinghouse on Handicapped and Gifted Children.

Seagoe, M. (1974). Some learning characteristics of gifted children. In R. Martinson (Ed.), *The identification of the gifted and talented.* Ventura, CA: Office of the Ventura County Superintendent of Schools.

Soltan, R. (2002). Precocious readers. *MLA Forum, 1(1).*

Strip, C., & Hirsch, G. (2000). *Helping gifted children soar: A practical guide for parents and teachers.* Scottsdale, AZ: Great Potential Press (formerly Gifted Psychology Press).

Tomlinson, C. (1995). *How to differentiate instruction in a mixed-ability classroom.* Alexandria, VA: Association for Supervision and Curriculum Development.

Tomlinson, C. (2001). *How to differentiate instruction in mixed-ability classrooms.* Alexandria, VA: Association for Supervision and Curriculum Development.

Valentino, C. (2000). *Flexible grouping.* Retrieved November 27, 2003, from www.eduplace.com/science/profdev/articles/valentino.html.

VanTassel-Baska, J. L. (1998). *Comprehensive curriculum for the gifted learner.* Boston: Allyn & Bacon.

Webb, J. T. (1994). *Nurturing social-emotional development of gifted children.* ERIC (EC #527). Arlington, VA: The ERIC Clearinghouse on Disabilities and Gifted Education.

Winebrenner, S. (2001). *Teaching gifted kids in the regular classroom* (2nd ed.). Minneapolis, MN: Free Spirit.

Index

About the Author

Teresa Masiello is a Gifted and Talented Resource Specialist for the public school system in Frederick County, Virginia. She has taught for 19 years at elementary and middle school levels. Teaching at these different grade levels has deepened her beliefs about the importance of appropriately selected literature for all students.

In addition to her many years as a teacher, Teresa's experience with gifted and talented children includes her role as a resource specialist, as a member of the gifted advisory committee, and as a parent. She has done many workshops and teacher in-service training sessions on teaching reading to gifted children. She currently works with gifted students in grades K-3. Teresa has also been an assistant coach with Destination Imagination® and has served on various instructional committees. In addition, she has written for *Gifted Education Press Quarterly*.

Teresa has an M.A. degree in Teaching from Shenandoah University. She holds endorsements in Administration, Supervision, and Gifted Education. Her undergraduate degree is from George Mason University in Virginia. When not busy working, she enjoys spending time with her husband, Paul, her 12-year-old son, Anthony, and her seven-year-old twins, Jacob and Nicole.